BY SCOTT ALLAN

BULLET PROOF

MINDSET MASTERY

THE SERIES

Bulletproof Mindset Mastery Series:

Vol.1: Books 1-2

JOIN THE COMMUNITY OF 30,000 LIFETIME LEARNERS!

Sign up today for my **free weekly newsletter** and receive instant access to **the <u>onboarding subscriber pack</u>** that includes:

The Fearless Confidence Action Guide: 9 Action Plans for Building Limitless Confidence and Achieving Sustainable Results!

The bestseller poster pack: A poster set of Scott Allan's bestselling books

The Zero Procrastination Blueprint: A Step-by-Step Blueprint to Turn Procrastination into Rapid Action Implementation!

Begin Your Journey and Make This Life Your Own.
Click Here to <u>Subscribe Today</u>, or scan the <u>QR code</u> below.

Bulletproof Mindset Mastery

Vol 1: Books 1-2

BREAK YOUR LIMITATIONS, CONQUER
RESISTANCE AND CRUSH NEGATIVE BEHAVIOR

BOOK 1: Nothing Scares Me
BOOK 2: Relaunch Your Life

SCOTT ALLAN

Scott Allan PUBLISHING
MASTER YOUR LIFE ONE BOOK AT A TIME

Contents

BULLET PROOF
BY SCOTT ALLAN
MINDSET MASTERY
THE SERIES

BULLETPROOF
MINDSET MASTERY

2 BOOKS IN 1

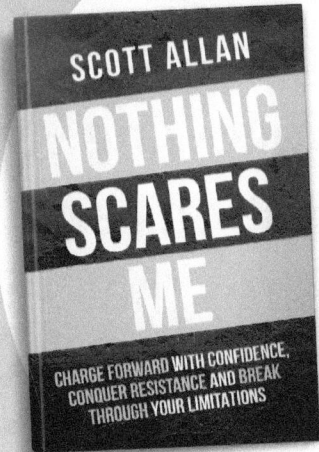

SCOTT ALLAN

NOTHING
SCARES
ME

CHARGE FORWARD WITH CONFIDENCE,
CONQUER RESISTANCE AND BREAK
THROUGH YOUR LIMITATIONS

CRUSH YOUR
NEGATIVE BEHAVIOR

RELAUNCH
YOUR LIFE

BREAK THE CYCLE
OF SELF-DEFEAT,
DESTROY NEGATIVE
EMOTIONS, AND
RECLAIM YOUR
PERSONAL POWER

SCOTT ALLAN

SCOTT ALLAN

"**Mastery** is not a question of genetics of luck, but of following your natural inclinations and the deep desires that stir you from within."

—Robert Greene

Introduction: Bulletproof Mindset Mastery, Vol. 1

*Do your internal fears hold you back from taking immediate action? Do you want to reinvent your life but don't know where to begin? Want to **overcome fear and uncertainty** while putting an end to the negative behaviors blocking you from living the life you desire?*

If the answer is yes, the time is now for you to say NO to the fear, negative emotions, and unresolved issues blocking you from becoming your personal best.

International Best-selling author and High-Performance Mastery coach Scott Allan has put together two of his bestselling books in one value-packed combo-pack to increase your maximum performance. These books are guaranteed to help you achieve the results you need to become unbreakable, unbeatable and undefeatable.

The **Bulletproof Mindset Mastery** "2 books in 1" combo-pack includes:

Nothing Scares Me

In *Nothing Scares Me*, you'll build an immunity to fearful situations that once baffled you. By taking action in the face of fear, you will end the self-doubt holding you back and create a thriving, **undefeated,** and **fearless** lifestyle.

Nothing Scares Me will show you how to:

- Make intentional decisions and take back control of your life

- Let go of excuses stopping you from moving forward

- Turn negative thoughts into positive choices

- Transform bad habits keeping you stuck

- Build unbreakable confidence by taking consistent action

Nothing Scares Me is a book that challenges your fears and pushes you to overcome the resistance to change. You will learn specific strategies to develop a limitless mindset while putting an end to limiting beliefs.

Relaunch Your Life

Relaunch Your Life takes you by the hand and guides you through the four mindsets failing you. You will learn strategies for overcoming social awkwardness, eliminating your fear of rejection, and ending the negative behaviors holding you back.

In *Relaunch Your Life,* you will discover how to...

- Break the cycle of self-defeat keeping you trapped

- Confront your fears of vulnerability

- Get over your feelings of isolation and social exclusion

- Achieve greater satisfaction in your personal and business relationships

- Create a master vision for your life and build a blueprint for success

Relaunch Your Life is the only book you need to **overcome fear and uncertainty** while putting an end to the harmful behaviors blocking you from living the life you want.

This 2-book compilation series is a practical blueprint that introduces specific strategies, action-based tasks, and ground-breaking material strategically created to give you the ultimate edge for success and develop your mind for high-performance success in everything you do.

SCOTT ALLAN

NOTHING SCARES ME

CHARGE FORWARD WITH CONFIDENCE, CONQUER RESISTANCE AND BREAK THROUGH YOUR LIMITATIONS

Nothing
Scares Me

CHARGE FORWARD WITH CONFIDENCE,
CONQUER RESISTANCE, AND BREAK THROUGH
YOUR LIMITATIONS

by Scott Allan

"Fear is good. Like self-doubt, fear is an indicator. Fear tells us what we have to do. Remember our rule of thumb: the more scared we are of a work or calling, the more sure we can be that we have to do it."

— *Steven Pressfield,* *Author of* The War of Art

Nothing Scares Me: A Message from the Author

Hi there, I'm **Scott Allan**, the author of *Nothing Scares Me*, and before we dive into this content, I need five minutes of your time to explain a few things about the book, and how it's emerged as one of my greatest works in the past five years.

The journey to conquer fear and all its psychological complexities has always fascinated me, for the most part because, there is a direct correlation between being scared and taking intentional action anyway. I noticed this back in 1997 when, the fear of doing anything always led to massive procrastination, followed by a tsunami of excuses that justified all the reasons why I couldn't do something.

I had a lot of ambition, but your dreams can be clouded by the fear of failure and the unknown when you let the fear in and keep courage locked out.

So, this began as a competition. Instead of giving into the fear and taking the lesser path, I would ask myself in the moment of fear: "What if I just take one small step? What if I take one tiny action towards the one thing I fear doing? What could happen?"

As my favorite author on this subject, the late Susan Jeffers has said, "We must feel the fear...and do it anyway!"

So, based on this advice, I started doing that. I began to do things that scared me anyway. What changed as a result?

As It turns out, **everything**.

A lot of people claim to have the secret sauce to defeating fear and doing miraculous things but, as a recovering fear addict who needs to keep things simple, the best strategy I learned to employ was just "Do it Anyway!"

As it happens (and I discuss in the book you're about to read), taking action builds momentum. It aligns the universe with your dreams, ambitions, and goals. You begin to realize that the fear will never go away, but is always there when we are challenged to try something new.

If your never scared in life, it could be because you're not doing anything to move to that next level.

My challenge to you is, always be scared. If it's true that people with big goals are the most frightened, set a goal so impossible to achieve that it will astonish you when you reach your destination.

I did this years ago, and twenty years later I had traveled the world, written 20+ books, and living my dreams—only because every morning I would wake up with that one big question: "What can I do today that scares me?"

Visualize the outcome as you take direct action and, regardless if you hit your target or not, it's better than standing still and doing nothing.

A Shift from the Previous Title

This book was previously titles **Do It Scared**, but with the popularity of this title appearing in other books over the years, we decided to shift away and give this book a new beginning with *Nothing Scares Me*.

The content is still the same as when it was originally published in 2017, but with a better cover and stronger appeal for a new audience that is set to crush fear and build big dreams.

Let's move forward. When you wake up, start each morning with the one simple phrase: Nothing Scares Me!

In memory of the fearless leader Susan Jeffers, let's face the fear together...and do it anyways!

Scott Allan

The Forces Holding You Back

"I have learned over the years that when one's mind is made up, this diminishes fear; knowing what must be done does away with fear."

— Rosa Parks

Imagine for a moment there is something you want so badly that it hurts to go without it. Maybe you've tried to grab that dream as it dangles in front of you, but it keeps escaping your grasp.

When people say *take direct action and just do it*, you find yourself too paralyzed to do anything. Instead, you find yourself reaching for a remote control, or killing time by immersing yourself in things that just entertain you.

As a result, you've settled for a life of good enough, and opted to live in fear

The *fear of not doing what you want to do, fear of living without,* and *the fear of growing old and never taking a chance on your future.*

Now, imagine that an invisible force is holding you back from having this one thing. It is so powerful that, no matter how hard you try to break free, it won't let you go.

That force is **fear**.

It is powerful, and for most people it is the single largest cause of self-defeat.

But, unlike most obstacles that are easy to identify, what keeps you scared is more difficult to see. We are blinded by the forces in our lives that trap us because we assume life is supposed to be this way.

When something is risky, we make excuses for why we shouldn't do it. Then, when a good opportunity presents itself, we say, *maybe next time*. But when next time arrives, there is always another excuse.

Many of us have trained ourselves to avoid the scary stuff in life, and instead, we settle for what is easy and less risky. The fear of scarcity has taken over the beauty of abundance. The result is, you create a life where you are clinging to the things that don't matter when you should be letting go.

Why Do We Trap Ourselves?

We hold ourselves back for many reasons: fear of failure, not being able to measure up, or trying to avoid looking stupid. So instead of **doing something about it**, we do nothing at all and life passes us by. Then one day you turn 50 years old. You realize you don't have much time left and you're stuck in a job, a relationship, or a situation that would have been different if you had confronted and acted on the fears that were shaping your life.

Well...

I have good news and bad news. The good news is, it's never too late to start doing the work you've always wanted to do. The bad news is, those moments you missed can never be reclaimed. But don't worry about that now. We have this day and the rest of our lives, however long that may be, to make a difference, change our behavior, take intentional action, and do the things we've always dreamed of.

From now on, you have two choices: you can either take intentional action, or do nothing at all. One path can bring you everything you've ever wanted. The other will continue to bring you more of what you've always had.

You are being held back by something that is not beyond your control. It is the result of years of conditioning and old beliefs that feed into negative thoughts about who you really are. You've been lying to yourself about how great you can be.

This doesn't have to be you anymore. We all have choices we can make in any given moment. When you think you have no choice, you are making a choice to believe that and in doing so, you're limiting your opportunities to taking the scraps left over by everyone else that got there first.

Do you want to spend the rest of your days wondering: *"What if I had...?"*

This brings us to the all-important question: Is it really life we are afraid of? Or are we just afraid to be ourselves in this life?

By the time you finish this book, you'll be doing the things you once only dreamed of. If there is any one tragedy, it is watching people live their lives in mediocrity when they have the desire to shine.

But, nobody talks about the shining greatness they could achieve. We bury what we feel passionate about because we have been told dreams are for kids. We have been told to grow up and face reality.

When we reach adulthood, it is time to get real, get an education, and get a job. I've done all these things, and even though I have no big regrets, I know that if I had stayed scared and not pursued my journey, one day I would have the biggest regret of all: I would reach the end of my life and realize that I did very little to change it.

You can change it. It is never too late to start. Life is short. Let's not waste it by staying small. There is no great fulfillment in living just half a life.

The Secret to Taking Action When Scared

When you hear about others doing things you want to do, does a pang of jealousy run through you? Don't you just want to call them up and say, "So what is your secret anyway? How is it that you did this and I didn't? What makes you better than me? What do you have that I don't?"

We often overestimate other people's abilities because it helps us deal with our feelings of failure and underachievement. When we label ourselves as failures, feelings of shame creep in. But you are not a failure. The fight isn't over until you say it is. You haven't lost anything until you decide it is time to give up. I'm betting you aren't ready to do that yet.

That is why you're here. To figure out what it is you want and how to get it. And to get it, you have to do something about your situation, life, and lifestyle. It is common for people to reach a stage in life when they look around and say, "Wait. I don't want any of this? What am I doing this for?"

Trust me. You are not alone. If you are questioning the life you have been handed, this is a good thing. It is the first step to changing it. Many people don't take that first step. They don't stop long enough to question why.

Consider this question:

How much confidence would you need to do the one thing you've always wanted to do?

In other words, *how much courage would you need to live your dream and do the things that scare you and are keeping you trapped?*

The truth is that you don't need bravery or courage. This is the illusion of confidence. For years, I believed that before I could do anything I had to be completely skilled at it so I could perform without failing. There are a lot of things we should prepare for, but perfection and being good enough before we start holds us back from doing it in the first place.

This belief that before we try it, we have to be totally perfect, full of confidence, and bursting with courage is one of the biggest lies that keeps us from doing anything, scared or not. When we are not feeling any of these things, and when we lack confidence to take action, what do we do? Something else. But the secret is so obvious that I'm sure you know it already.

It isn't confidence that comes first, but taking action. Confidence follows action. You do it first and then the confidence comes. We act first and then experience courage later.

The Path to Reinvention

Reinventing yourself takes time. Although change can happen instantly, consistent change that takes place over an extended period of time will have a lasting effect that sticks. In the end, we want habits and rituals that stick after the transformation takes place.

This book is one of the pathways to that reinvention. When I look back on my life and I see all that I have done [and haven't yet], part of me lingers on the idea that I could have done so much more if I hadn't been afraid. Yes, staying scared and retreating from fear kills dreams. And because we don't want to face the truth of how scared we really are, the excuses and justifications come and we think:

- *Oh, I didn't want that opportunity anyway. I'll wait for the next one.*
- *Success is overrated. It's better to stay average and not push yourself too far.*
- *The chances of making it in that competition are too low; I am not going to try something I'm sure to fail.*

Making excuses and coming up with reasons to fail are the biggest reason people don't empower themselves to take immediate action when scared. Instead, we stay scared and settle for the life that *is* instead of the life that *could be*.

As a result, we grow into a lifestyle that is waiting to deliver emotional pain in the form of regret. This is:

- The pain of knowing what you could have become if you had the courage to do the things that scared you.
- The pain of doing work you hate instead of work you love.
- The pain of making friends with people who support your life of average mediocrity because they too are scared.

The lies we tell ourselves come at a heavy price. You are paying that price a little bit every day when you stay scared and choose to do nothing. *Nothing Scares Me* is designed to get you moving toward the dreams you've buried for too long.

Consider these questions:

1. Are you where you want to be in your life today? If you answered no, would you like to be in the same place one year from now?
2. Did you have a vision for your life that brought you to the stage you're at right now? If not, do you have a vision for the next year? Can you clearly see where you are going and how you are going to get there?
3. Can you see yourself taking action to remove the biggest obstacle in your life today?
4. Are you terrified of doing this one thing? If so, what are you going to do to overcome this fear?

Life is an adventure to be lived, but sadly, many people are not living the life they dream of. Instead we are lost in the crowd of souls waking up and doing work we don't like because somewhere along the way we chose the easy path.

I don't know a lot but I do know this: our lives are short, and some are shorter than others. Much shorter. This is why we must appreciate every day.

You were brought into this world for a reason. Aren't you the least bit curious to know what it is? I know I am, and I try to uncover a bit of this treasure every day. I try to discover something new and do what part of me may want to resist creating more abundance in my life and the lives of others.

We all have reasons for staying scared, but this doesn't mean we have to like it. In this book, I will share strategies and case studies I have used to get over my fear of taking action.

When you run from fear, you take it with you. There's no escape. You cannot change or reinvent anything until you throw yourself over that hurdle of life.

Now, are you ready to empower your fear and take action today no matter how scared you are?

Let's do it...and change the way things are for the rest of your life.

See you on the inside.

Scott Allan

Aim High for Your Vision of Impossibility

"So many of our dreams at first seem impossible, then they seem improbable, and then, when we summon the will, they soon become inevitable."

— Christopher Reeve

I believe in the power of impossibility. When someone says it can't be done I immediately think: *You are right. It can't be, not by you, and not with that attitude, but I'll give it a try.* However, as history has shown, impossibilities are only as real as the power we give them.

As Henry Ford once said, "Whether you think you can, or think you can't – you're right."

You don't have to change the world, but if you want to change yourself, your circumstances, or your current situation, you'll have to develop the habit of doing things that scare you.

This isn't as hard as it sounds. In fact, if you look back on your life I'm sure you'll find lots of times when you took a chance and did something when you were full of fear. You knew at that time that it had to be done no matter the outcome. You knew that pushing forward was the only way.

When we intentionally invite fear into our lives, it creates a level of discomfort that many of us are not used to. When you trust in what seems impossible, even when it pushes your current limiting beliefs, you are laying the foundation for a life of impossible dreams and circumstances.

Take a look around. Do you know someone who has created the life you crave by pushing their courage to do something most people would consider an impossibility? All successful people I know have a small band of supporters on one side and doubters on the other. People who live in fear are fearful of watching others succeed. If the impossible can be accomplished, it proves that our excuses are no longer valid.

When we no longer hold onto an excuse to validate why we can't do something, it opens the doors of possibility. Anything can be accomplished. We can break through any barrier and overcome adversity.

People who dream about success but do not take action are only dreamers. They spend their lives admiring what others have achieved and, this fills them with envy for what they could have had.

You have two choices: you can dream about it and do nothing to make it happen. Or, you can make it happen by doing something about it and then start to live your dream.

Crafting a vision and executing a plan is the best way to get to where you want to be. A life without a vision will rarely move beyond mediocre. If we stay within mediocre boundaries, we risk staying scared. If we stay scared, we become too paralyzed with fear to take any action.

Pushing Past Negative Self-Talk

We have all been there: you desire to be at a certain level but repeatedly tell yourself you can't get there. You want to believe but the voices of doubt and internal critics make you believe a different story.

Negative self-talk feeds us the "truth" about who we are and what we can do. But more often than not, what we believe isn't necessarily the truth. Our thoughts and internal beliefs just make it so.

But remember this: Your inner voices are not in control of your thoughts, actions, or behavior. You are.

When we listen to the negative voices that fill us with self-doubt, we believe the messages we receive. Who are we to doubt the voices in our own minds? Who are we to think so little of ourselves that we unconsciously decide to stay small by choice?

If you were to slow down right now and listen to the thoughts running through your head, you would be able to recognize the conversation that is running rampant. It sounds like a symphony of politicians arguing over the next tax increase.

Most of the time we operate on autopilot. But our thoughts turn into words and, those words create visual images. Your mind is powerful and can make you believe anything through this one-way conversation.

Who is controlling this conversation? You are. When you recognize that you are in control of your thoughts, you can take full responsibility for the outcome of events.

When these thoughts lead to negative words thrown about in anger, there is nobody else present to blame. It is just you. The mind takes over and tells you what you think you already know. But the truth is, we don't know what we don't know. So, we convince ourselves that what we believe must be true.

A mind filled with self-doubt creates a massive obstacle to maneuver around. Your doubt deepens your own limitations and beliefs about what is possible.

Most people, surprisingly, limit what they can do based on the doubts, opinions and limiting beliefs of others. When our peers, colleagues, or friends say that something isn't possible, the initial seed of doubt is planted in the mind.

We begin to question everything: *What if they are right? What if I fail and have to go back to the beginning? What if this makes me look bad? What if I don't have what it takes?*

When we fail to try, we never discover what we can really do. Our failure at not doing it becomes the obstacle. How do you know if you can't do something if you don't give it a shot? If you try you might fail, but it's better than doing nothing. The only way to know anything is to take a chance on doing it. If it doesn't work out, try it again using a different tactic.

You could be running these scenarios through your mind in thinking, "Who am I to...

- *Start my own business online?*
- *Travel around the world?*
- *Write a book?*
- *Earn one million dollars this year doing what I love?*
- *Quit my day job and pursue my life's passion?*
- *Deliver a keynote speech in front of thousands of people?*
- *Give up my compulsive addictions?*
- *Find the person I want to spend the rest of my life with?*
- *Journey to every country in the world?*
- *Win the Pulitzer Prize?*

People always doubt what they cannot do themselves. They fear what others can accomplish and what they themselves have failed to follow through on. But the people who achieve their goals and make dreams happen aren't lucky. They know what they want, they focus on how to get it, and then they charge forward and work until they succeed.

Don't let self-doubt stand in your way. Recognize it as the lie it is.

In actuality, it's not the negative influencers that plant the seeds of doubt in our minds that keep us from making our impossible dreams real. But rather, we do this to ourselves by subconsciously replaying the negative messages that keep us tied down. When you internalize their beliefs, this becomes your reality.

There are several key elements successful people have in common. It isn't genius, talent, or luck, although these factors play a role in being successful. Within the mind of every successful person there is a tenacious perseverance and the unbreakable belief that they are going to succeed no matter what.

Successful people struggle with doubt just like everyone else, but they have broken past it and keep pushing. Breaking the resistance is about doing what scares you even when you want to turn around and run the other way.

The difficult path is the journey. When you try to take shortcuts or do it easy, you will waste time doing work that doesn't matter. Hard work won't guarantee you success if you are working on the wrong things.

This is what we need to do if we are to face the fear of doing anything: **Continue to push forward** even when it's hard. When the going gets tough, you have to keep going.

People tend to get stuck when the way becomes difficult. During these times we have to reach out for help. Try to go it alone and you could isolate yourself, become frustrated and stop taking any risks at all. You might miss out on that opportunity or once-in-a-lifetime chance by doing it alone.

Let's take a look at Jim Carrey's story...

Years before he received a twenty-million-dollar paycheck for the movie *The Cable Guy*, Jim Carrey was doing stand-up comedy and working odd jobs to survive. But, he knew what he wanted. In fact, he was so sure of himself and his dream that he wrote a check to himself for ten million dollars and put it in his wallet.

Jim said he would walk around with it and visualize his life as a successful, highly paid actor. Several years later, Jim Carrey was holding a check for seven million dollars that he earned for *Dumb and Dumber*. Then he was paid twenty million for *The Cable Guy*. When Jim Carrey's father passed away, he slipped the check into the coffin to be buried.

Now, you might be thinking: *I don't have Jim Carrey's talent.* No, maybe you don't. He is Jim Carrey. You are you, and what you have, belongs to you. This makes you unique. Your talents, abilities, and gifts are unique. If you don't know what they are yet, that's okay. Keep searching. This takes time and there are no shortcuts.

But what you can do is imagine the impossible. See your life as it could be in five years. Put yourself in the future, visualize what you will be doing, and imagine how happy you are to be where you are.

Then, come back to the present and write down a series of action plans and tasks to get yourself there. This is how you overcome the tough obstacles in your way. When you know what you want, taking on fear and **taking intentional action** ceases to be a problem and becomes part of the process.

But, for your impossible dream to come true, you have to do two things:

1. **Be willing to do the things that scare you**. What is holding you back? What do you resist? What do you believe in? Are you repeating negative self-talk that keeps you stuck in a rut?

2. **Execute your plan.** It takes work, perseverance, and a plan to make your dream come true. What action steps can you take right now? How can you make your time more productive? Do you deal with action paralysis? What doubts stop you from moving forward?

Making Your Impossible Dreams a Reality

Take a moment to think about all the cool inventions, gadgets, and technology we have today. For a small fee, you can fly to places around the world and visit exotic locations. At the push of a button, you can instantly connect with an old friend who lives thousands of miles away. Grab a set of keys and you can drive to another state in just a few hours.

It seems like, in today's world, nothing is impossible. And yet, just one hundred years ago people could never have imagined what is possible today. It took the courage of some brave men and women to blaze the trail for the world.

As we think about the impossible possibilities that exist and surround us today, is it realistic to have limitations? Don't they exist only in our minds? If a young engineer can design an app that changes the world, why isn't anything possible? Yet, many people are scared to do what they want to do for fear of...

Failing. Yes, failure is part of the journey. It isn't something we should avoid but embrace. Most people would rather stay stuck in a job they hate for a paycheck than face the failure of doing something different.

Someone I know once said to me: "Whatever dreams I had ended when I settled for the comfort of reality."

I don't know about you but reality for me is doing what I have always been frightened to do. When you take action and do the things that our minds are telling us not to do because it is too risky, that is a signal that you are being held back.

There are many times we are challenged to do more than is expected. Watch for these opportunities and don't let them get away.

The fear of failure keeps us from pursuing our impossible dreams. Yet, great men and woman for centuries have challenged the impossible and did exactly what they set out to achieve. It doesn't matter if you're training for the Olympics, you can still do what scares you and make it happen if you want it.

If you **really** want it.

Do you want to quit your job in two years and work full time from home? You can do it if you put in the work. In two years, the impossible dream will be yours.

Do you want to create a product that helps people live better, higher-quality lives? You can do it.

How about traveling the world as a digital nomad and making a living from your online platform? It is totally possible. Rob Cubbon of http://robcubbon.com does exactly that, traveling throughout Southeast Asia while connecting with his readers through his blog, videos and online courses.

Maybe you're stuck in a painful place in your life. Maybe you want to move forward. Maybe you want to take massive action but don't know what to do. Or, maybe you want to be somebody different, but you can't let go of the person you've always been. Does it sound too good to be true?

I know, but remember that ordinary people do extraordinary things every day. They always have and always will. Someone once said to me, "All the good stuff has already been done." That's a limiting belief I don't agree with. The world always has room for another book, a new song, or a product that can improve the quality of life.

Inspire Your Passion

Colonel Sanders didn't achieve his success until he was nearly 65. For years, he tried to sell his recipe but nobody was interested. Now there are over 20,000 Kentucky Fried Chicken restaurants in 125 countries and territories around the world.

Author **JK Rowling** had the idea for Harry Potter while delayed on a train. She spent the next five years planning out the seven books of the series. JK Rowling was broke and nearly homeless by the time a publisher finally picked up the book. Relentlessly she pursued her impossible dream until it came true. Now over 400 million copies of the Harry Potter books have been sold worldwide, making her the first author to reach billionaire status.

Henry Ford had a dream to see every family in America able to afford a car. So, he created the assembly line to manufacture cars at a rate of 1,000 a day. Soon, half of the cars in the world were Fords.

Ray Kroc was a milkshake-device salesman before purchasing McDonald's at the age of 52 in 1954. He built it into the world's largest fast-food franchise, with his global vision of a McDonald's restaurant in every town and city across America.

Jerry Seinfeld was once booed offstage as a stand-up comic. He could have quit, but instead he returned to that same stage and, **tapping into the "Nothing Scares Me" mindset**, succeeded in becoming one of the most famous comedians with one of the highest ranked TV shows in history: *Seinfeld*.

It's never too late, and it's never impossible. It never has been. Impossible dreams are happening all around us. The difference between having what you want and giving up what you want is the belief that anything is possible. Only our thinking makes it real.

People who take intentional action, even when they are scared, can achieve amazing results in a short period of time. But sharing their dreams with others and being laughed at is what holds many people back.

What, you? A sport star?

What, you? A famous novelist?

What, you? Running for president?

What, you? A millionaire?

I know. I've heard it all before. Yet, these same people are living mediocre lives and doing nothing extraordinary except collecting paychecks. There is nothing impossible about that.

I've listened to naysayers most of my life. Many times I believed what they told me. It held me back for years. But I have no one to blame but myself if I do nothing to change my situation.

So, let's dream wildly, and break through our limits by smashing negative thoughts. Kick them out of your life and don't let them come back.

What Scares You That Must Be Done?

We all have dreams. Even if you aren't sure what it is yet, it is there. I don't know what yours are, but I've known mine for a long time. And I think that if you don't know what your purpose is, or you think you have nothing great to contribute to the world, you haven't dug deep enough. It's there. You need to find it. If you don't, you risk spending the rest of your life at the mercy of someone else and their choices. In my opinion, that's the worst way to live scared -- when somebody or something decides how you should live.

Nobody chooses your path but you.

So, pull the trigger and make key choices that will impact your life for the rest of your days to come. And most importantly, choose the people who will walk it with you.

As we will see in the next chapter, the people you hang out with will either help you get to where you want to go, or they will stop you from getting there. Good company on the journey is everything.

What do you want that really scares you? In most cases, our dreams are frightening versions of a reality that we see as far, far away in another land that we can't imagine. But look at what people are doing every day. Twenty years ago, there was no social media, and now we can connect with millions of people from our own homes. Billion-dollar companies have been built and are thriving because someone had a vision and they brought it to life.

How did they do this? By believing in an impossible dream.

Did they have moments of self-doubt and fear? Certainly. But this is why we are here, to break through what holds us back, to get to where we need to be in our life. When your dream really scares you, you could be on the right path. Don't think of the fear is a warning but rather a sign that this is the way you were meant to travel.

Key Takeaways

Right now, take out a piece of paper and a pen. I want you to do a short exercise. Write down what you know to be your impossible vision of success. Whatever it is, stretch your imagination. Make it larger than life. No, bigger than that! Go large.

- If you are a writer, do you want to sell a few books, or millions of books?
- If you are working for a company, do you want to collect a paycheck, or to be the one who starts up the company of his or her dreams?
- If your passion is music, can you imagine yourself playing in front of a sold-out crowd in Las Vegas?

- Next, write down three obstacles in your life that scare you. What are they? If you can only come up with one, that is fine. Focus just on that.
- Then, write down your ideas for tackling this fear. What is the single most important step you could take right now that would get you moving towards your impossible dream?
- Now, what are you going to do scared today? Try to do just one thing that scares you. Don't wait for it to come to you. Go after it.

The Ostrich Effect and Embracing Reality

"Just as we develop our physical muscles through overcoming opposition - such as lifting weights - we develop our character muscles by overcoming challenges and adversity."

—Stephen Covey, author of *The 7 Habits of Highly Effective People*

The Ostrich Effect was originally coined by Galai and Sade to describe investor attempts to avoid negative financial information. When times were tough and the market was crashing, people who looked the other way and pretended everything was fine stood to risk losing their entire fortunes.

To avoid bad news or the discomfort of facing a negative situation, many people turned to entertainment devices, addictions and various methods of escapism as a means to cope. When everything was going to hell, they looked away and acted as if it would be okay.

When you bury your head in the sand to avoid the reality of a difficult situation, you risk losing everything.

If we take the Ostrich Effect and apply it to our own lives, we can spot the situations that we ignore every day. By avoiding responsibility in one area, say, for example, a bad marriage, we can avoid the discomfort of dealing with it.

By running away from reality, we can dodge a bullet and hope that we don't get hit, but it rarely works this way. Just like the investors that decide not to monitor their fortune when the market spins, we make similar choices in our own lives. These decisions can lead to emotional or financial disaster.

The Ostrich Effect is a powerful form of personal manipulative persuasion. It goes without saying that *you can run but you can't hide.* When faced with a frightening challenge, we look for someone else to carry the burden or take responsibility, and meanwhile, we create all kinds of reasons why we shouldn't take action.

Here are some examples:

When a **relationship turns toxic**, we pretend everything is okay. If we just keep our heads down and don't rock the boat, things will improve. You're in a relationship that has turned emotionally abusive, but you stick with it, telling yourself it'll get better. The worse it gets, the harder you try to pretend it will work out.

When we are **thousands of dollars in debt**, and can barely pay the monthly minimum on our credit cards, we pretend the problem doesn't exist and keep on spending. You are in debt, you have no money, and the bank is calling. You turn off your phone and head out for one last shopping spree. Months later you are bankrupt and wondering what happened.

When our **health is on the line** and the doctor has warned us of the inherent danger of smoking, we keep on doing it, ignoring the warning signs of illness. We are overweight and the doctor warned us of the health risks. Yet, we continue to shovel in the junk food and stick with a fast food diet.

Each of these situations looks and feels hopeless. You may experience one or all of these. But there are choices we can make to deal with the massive obstacles that hold us back.

You have to be ready to see the obstacles for what they are. You have to want to change and face the reality of what is happening. Only by confronting your fears can they be removed.

The Stockdale Paradox

James Stockdale was a United States Vice Admiral who was shot down in 1965 and held as a prisoner of war in Vietnam for over seven years. While captive he was routinely tortured and made to undergo some of the harshest treatments any person could endure.

When asked how he made it through alive, while other prisoners around him died, Stockdale said:

"Oh, that's easy, the optimists. Oh, they were the ones who said, 'We're going to be out by Christmas.' And Christmas would come, and Christmas would go. Then they'd say, 'We're going to be out by Easter.' And Easter would come, and Easter would go. And then Thanksgiving, and then it would be Christmas again. And they died of a broken heart."

It goes without saying that confronting the brutal facts of your reality, no matter how terrifying, is smarter that convincing yourself it is all okay when in your heart you know it really isn't.

So why do so many of us hide from the truth? Why do we choose a path of living in fear instead of confronting reality?

Jim Collins, the bestselling author of *Good to Great*, interviewed James Stockdale who went on to say:

"It comes down to faith: knowing that no matter what, you will make it through to the other side. Nobody can promise that you'll win or come out okay. You might lose everything. It is having the faith that you are strong enough to get through the worst parts of your life, whatever it may be, and that you will prevail in the end. This can only happen when you face the most brutal facts of your current reality."

Reading the story of James Stockdale, a man who had nothing left but the iron will of his own faith and a solid belief he would prevail no matter what, sets a new precedent for how we should handle impossible situations.

If James Stockdale made it through the worst hell imaginable and maintained an unbreakable faith that he would survive no matter what, what is to stop the rest of us from overcoming insurmountable difficulties?

Viktor Frankl

In a similar situation, many years earlier in October 1944 during World War II, a man named Viktor Frankl was sent to the Auschwitz concentration camp. During his imprisonment, Frankl observed death as part of daily life. He watched men succumb to their fate, often at his own feet.

In his book, *Man's Search for Meaning,* Viktor E. Frankl describes his experience in the camps, how he confronted the horrors of those days, and more importantly, how he survived:

"The experiences of camp life show that man does have a choice of action. There were always choices to make. Every day, every hour, offered the opportunity to make a decision, a decision which determined whether you would or would not submit to those powers which threatened to rob you of your very self, your inner freedom."

Therein lies the solution to either living like an ostrich or facing life with the courage of a lion; you think you have no choice, but that is a lie. You always have a choice, regardless of your current situation, in how you respond and, more importantly, how you take action.

What will you do when faced with adversity? Will you search inside yourself to discover your faith that everything will work out no matter what happens? Or will you doom yourself to a fate of hopelessness and just accept whatever comes your way by default?

Facing the reality of our current situation certainly is not easy. In the most extreme of conditions, such as the stories I just mentioned, it is life or death.

In our day-to-day life, we are forced to make decisions we don't want to make that often involve sacrifice, loss, or heartbreak. We want to procrastinate and put them off until tomorrow. We're tempted to keep busy doing other things that matter less to avoid the big issues pressing down on our lives now.

Every day we can be faced with situations that are hard, challenging, scary, or down-right terrifying. You might be going through a divorce, bankruptcy, or have recently lost a loved one. Most of us, if we are honest with ourselves, don't want to face the brutal reality of what is happening, and so we tell ourselves little lies.

These little lies come at a price: they keep you trapped. Before you realize what is happening, the situation is beyond your control. In **Nothing Scares Me**, we stand up to what scares us, no matter how bad it may be. We want to develop a faith that is unbreakable. We want to believe that no matter what, we can get through this and that we can handle whatever comes.

Here are some of the lies we tell ourselves that, as much as we would like to believe them, will bring us more pain in the long run:

- It'll work out somehow. [Reality: In other words, if I do nothing, some miracle will occur and someone will pay off my crushing debt].
- If I do nothing, somebody else will take care of it. [Reality: I created this situation, but by pretending it doesn't exist, I control my fear].
- The situation isn't as bad as I think. [Reality: It's usually worse].
- I'll fake it until I make it. [Reality: most people don't make it].

When we take the ostrich approach, like pretending that it's not as bad as we think, we are putting our lives in someone else's hands. That is a dangerous move to make. Putting your life into the hands of forces you cannot control is not a strategic plan. If you are not in control of your life and making intentional decisions about how you should be living, somebody else is.

Remember, nobody has your best interests at heart more than you do. The only guarantee you have is to put your life in good hands: your own. If, for whatever reason, you don't trust your own decision-making skills, your emotional state is fragile, or you're lacking confidence, I suggest finding someone, such as a good friend or mentor, to help you.

3 Steps to Building Rock-Solid Faith in Your Future

Make Your Commitment. Decide what you are committed to achieving and then work towards fulfilling that goal. People lose faith when they have nothing to strive for or look forward to having, being, or doing. A life without a future is dim and you will lose hope.

Stay Grounded in Reality. We can lose sight of our own reality when illusion and fantasy take over. This happens when we view reality as suffering. Let's face it: nobody wants to go through emotional trauma or suffer needlessly. But life is full of hard times. Relationships, careers, and health are always transforming. Nothing stays the same.

We lose our sense of reality when we pretend everything is okay without doing anything about it. You have to get realistic about your situation. This empowers your faith that, no matter what, this situation will pass.

Everything passes eventually. Nothing stays the same. Condition your mind to stay focused on the reality of your current state and be aware of what is happening, not what you think it should be. Then...

Reflect on Past Difficulties. What situations have you struggled with, but survived, in the past? Take a trip back through time and remember these events. Do you remember how you felt at the time? Did you think it would never end?

It's a common misperception that times of difficulty will last forever. You think to yourself: *I'll never get through this.* But you do. Take note of the stuff you've gone through that is now behind you.

By reflecting on past triumphs, we can discover faith that everything, no matter how bad it really is or seems, can be overcome. We will prevail in the end.

Key Takeaways

It is time to get realistic about the reality of your situation.

What you avoid will never go away. What we hide from eventually finds us. You end up missing out on opportunity, losing valuable relationships, or, holding onto things that tear us down when we fail to recognize them.

Are you avoiding a bad marriage, confronting a bad investment, or a situation at work that continues to get worse?

When we turn away from reality, we invite a life of fantasy and illusion. Is there an illusion you are stuck in? What are you avoiding that needs to be done? Is there anything you've been putting off? If so, why? Identifying the reason why you are avoiding something takes away its power. It gives you opportunity to create a solution.

Make a commitment to confronting your fear. Stay grounded in the reality of your situation. When things go bad, ask yourself how you can handle the situation. What are you *not* doing that could shift the outcome?

Remind yourself what your strengths are and tap into your power by focusing on this. The situation, no matter how bad it may be, only grows worse when you pretend it's not there.

Taking the First Leap from Ground Zero

Several years ago, I returned to Canada with my nine-year-old daughter for a two-week vacation. On this trip, I had an experience that changed everything, including the way I look at doing things even when I'm scared.

One day we set out to for a zip line tree adventure park. I don't know much about zip lining, but I was about to find out. After arriving we were quickly harnessed up, given a few instructions on how to use the equipment, and sent out for the adventure of a lifetime.

Just for the record, **I'm terrified of heights**.

We stayed mostly on the junior courses, practicing our zip lining no more than ten feet off the ground, which I was comfortable with. Looking through the forest at the other courses, I could see some of the other adventurers zip lining over open chasms with hundred foot drops. That was okay for them; I had no plans for that.

When my daughter became more confident, she chose to do the next level on the junior course. But while getting to the top of the first tree she had second thoughts and came back down. However, I was determined to show her it could be done. My exact words were: "You have to believe you can do it, even when you're scared."

I walked a tightrope, stepped across boards on a suspension bridge that moved constantly beneath my feet, and then swung from tree to tree on a rope thirty feet above the ground, and I made it nearly all the way to the end.

I have to admit that my fear of heights was being challenged, but not until the last part of the course. Before I continue with the story, I need to mention a few things about the rules. One is that if you run into trouble on the course, you have to yell for help. Then, a qualified instructor will come get you out of the tree.

The second rule is that if you yell for help more than three times, you will have to wear an orange hat that signals to the other instructors [and the other people on the course] that you need to be watched carefully.

I didn't want the orange hat.

At the end of the course was an eighty-foot zip line cable that crossed over a sixty-foot open chasm. I wasn't expecting that. My first instinct was to run. I looked for an emergency ladder down. Nothing. I tried to unhook both hooks and climb down when no one was looking. But we're not able to unhook both hooks at the same time. One is always permanently attached to the rope wire. In other words, I had two choices: jump, or yell for help.

Just Jump and Trust It Will Be Okay.

Two choices: do it or don't do it. We need to try at the very least to try at the challenges that stand before us. You might be scared to leap, but it's the moment before you jump that is the most frightening. Once you fully commit to going all out, your momentum will carry you the rest of the way.

I'll admit I was panicked. Fearing heights and suddenly finding myself in a situation that left me with no other choice but to take action. My daughter was on the ground looking up telling me to just "jump and get on with it." My legs were like rubber.

This is what fear does to you. It puts things in perspective. What I realized in that moment was that no matter how safe we feel, it is the safety zone of our little world that keeps us the most scared. I was no longer confident or courageous.

I was just scared. What if I jumped and something happened? What if I didn't jump and they had to pull me off the tree? Then another thought came to me: *what would happen if I jumped and made it to the other side? How would that feel?*

That is what I focused on. The *after* feeling of having succeeded. Up to that point I was focused on the worst-case scenario such as an accident, getting stuck halfway, or worse: Wearing that orange hat I could already see a couple other people walking around on the course with.

So, I just said, "To hell with it!" I leaped into open air and the world went with me. I zipped along, over the treetops, my feet dangling in open air and the feeling of nothing but empty space beneath me. I realized that a lot could change in a few seconds. Just moments ago, I was scared out of my mind, then I was doing the thing that scared me, and finally, in the end as my feet touched land, I knew I'd done it.

I did what I was afraid to do; the first few seconds were the worst. After that I was challenging what scared me the most. In reaching the other side, I had proven that being scared is okay. What you decide is going to determine how far you can go. If I had walked off the platform I would never have known. Later that day I found myself zip lining over larger valleys with drops of up to one hundred feet. I felt some tension but nothing like the scare I had on that first jump.

The **first jump** was the key. None of it would have been possible if I hadn't taken that first leap.

In life, this can go for anything such as taking up a new sport, writing a book for the first time, or starting a new relationship. If you back out before you begin, you'll always look back and think: *where would I be if only I had...?*

Now, you can apply this to any situation that scares you. Whatever you are afraid of doing in the moment can be overcome in a moment of decision. One action leads to another action. Your success in one area leads to greater success in other things.

For example:

- You want to start a new business, but you don't know where to begin? Start with the easiest step and move forward.
- You want to ask someone out on a date, but you're afraid they'll say no? Not asking them out will guarantee failure.
- You want to take an examination to get a certification in a new field of work but 90 percent of test takers fail? Go ahead and take it. What's the worst that can happen? It's better to be one of the 90 percent that failed than the 100 percent who never tried.

If we fail to take action to achieve the things we desire most, we miss out on greater opportunities down the road. You might be scared to try something now, but how will you feel if somebody else beats you to it and they succeed where you could have?

This is why, even when you're scared, you always have a choice: you can jump off the ledge or go home. If you are struggling to make the leap, just think about making it to the other side. Every time you jump, your confidence level moves up a notch.

When you back down and decide to do it next time, you face the risk of watching someone else do what you could have done, receiving what could have been yours, and living with greater confidence because of it.

Never give up your right to succeed. If you give up enough times, eventually you'll build up enough regret to last a lifetime.

Regret is painful. I know. There are many times I didn't act and now, years later, I wish had. But the past can't be changed so don't waste time focusing on what you didn't do, but on what you can and will do.

Succeeding at whatever it is you are going after, requires more than just determination or motivation. We are diving deeper than that. The people who succeed are just as scared to take action as anyone. But there is one difference: Scared people do it anyway.

They do it because they know that the fear is not going anywhere. You can't wait for courage to show up. That comes later on after you have taken action. Those that wait end up stalling and stay stuck in paralysis mode. Do you want to take action today, or not at all?

Albert E.N. Grey, author of *The Common Denominator of Success*, said: "Successful people are afraid too, but the difference is, they are willing to go the extra distance, and to do what others are afraid to do."

Susan Jeffers, the international bestselling author of *Feel the Fear and Do It Anyway*, said: "Remember that underlying all our fears is a lack of trust in ourselves."

This attitude makes a massive difference in the way we approach fear. When we feel fear, we make choices in the moment that decide the fate of everything. We choose to take action or not. You either want it or you don't. You can let yourself run away, or you can face the unknown and charge ahead.

We are surrounded by people doing things scared and succeeding. By recognizing what scares you, why it scares you, and what you are going to do about it, you become empowered to take on any challenge. Everything is difficult the first time. For many people it is easier to stay in our safe zones and avoid doing the scary stuff.

In many cases, we function from day to day without stopping to ask why? Why am I scared? Why do I give in to resistance every time? Why is everything such a struggle?

The struggle is the way. When we can push through the problems that keep us awake at night, and choose to fight as opposed to accepting the situation, we create the changes we want. Nothing happens unless you make it happen first.

Creating momentum requires force, and the strength of this force depends on your ability to take massive action and the intensity level of this action.

Creating Your 'Nothing Scares Me' Action List

After doing the things I was afraid of doing, and facing those situations I didn't want to deal with, I made a list of everything that scared me. I had forty-seven items that ranged from dealing with addictions to money issues and relationships.

As it turns out, I had a lot of "scared" issues I wasn't dealing with, and when I made a list of them I had this incredible feeling of relief, as if a part of me had been set free. I was tired of letting this fear stop me from living the way I wanted to.

While it's okay to be scared, allowing this fear to become an obstacle stopping me from taking massive action wasn't an option. So, I set out to tackle these issues and to live a scared-free lifestyle.

Action Plan

Your action plan now is to make your own list of 'scared' items you are afraid of. This can be anything from the fear of having a serious conversation with someone to paying your overdue credit card bill.

Set aside thirty minutes. Then, list out all the things you have been avoiding or are afraid of doing. This can involve anything from personal relationships to career moves. Just make a list of the challenges you know is holding you back. Whatever you resist should be on the list.

Here are a few of the items I had on my list:

- Interacting with people in a social environment.
- Going to the bank to pay a bill that was months overdue.
- Having that "talk" with my daughter.
- Asking for more time off work.
- Creating a yearly financial savings plan.

- Making an appointment with the doctor for that much needed health check.
- Resigning from my current job and pursuing a new profession.

After making your list, prioritize it from top to bottom. Ask yourself: *what can be done right now?* If there is anything that can be taken care of quickly, do it today. By crossing something off your list you'll get a boost of confidence and that makes it easier to move onto the next item.

For bigger items you can create an extensive list of mini action steps. For example, one of the things on my list was setting up a monthly savings plan, but this required multiple action steps. Feeling overwhelmed, I had to break it down into manageable chunks. By breaking it into several smaller steps, I was able to get it done.

We resist taking action towards our goal at times because we are afraid we will fail at achieving them. You might fail if you try, but you'll certainly fail if you don't.

So go ahead. Write down all of the obstacles, challenges and fears that are keeping you stuck today. Keep going until you have exhausted all of your ideas. By the time you are done, you'll have a list of unfinished tasks to get to work on.

The key is to take them one by one. Break each task down into smaller steps. Focus on the details of each one. By completing the work that has gone unfinished, you can push through the shame and fear of living with failure.

Key Takeaways

Your safety zone is a place of comfort that can keep you stuck. We have to commit to a goal that is larger than we are to break free from this zone.

We resist taking action towards our goals because we are afraid of failing to achieve them. What are you resisting right now?

What massive action steps could you take today to start building momentum? What is your current goal, and what action steps are you taking to accomplish your milestone?

We have a choice in every difficult situation. What choices are you making right now?

Do you know what scares you? Make a list of your fears. Then, next to each fear, write down an action step you are taking to overcome this fear.

The first jump is always the most frightening. What is your first leap going to be?

Partnering With the Right People

"If your emotional abilities aren't in hand, if you don't have self-awareness, if you are not able to manage your distressing emotions, if you can't have empathy and have effective relationships, then no matter how smart you are, you are not going to get very far."

— Daniel Goleman

There is a saying about the company you keep: "If you hang out with five idiots, you are the sixth idiot."

If you spend your time with five successful entrepreneurs, you are the sixth. Spend your time with five productivity gurus whose focus is on getting things done, you're the six. Spend your time with five complainers, and you're the sixth complainer.

You can tell a lot about someone by the company they keep, both in their personal lives and in their professional lives.

We subconsciously gravitate toward the crowd that fits into our version of reality. As we choose our crowds, we make choices about our destiny by choosing the people who will help to shape it. The person you become is in alignment with the people you attract and spend the most time with.

Take a look around you at the people you associate with every day. Do you talk like them? Think like them? Do you look up to them? This is your circle of powerful influence, and it will have a profound impact on your success or failure in the coming years.

My grandfather once said to me, "You'll only reach the summit of the tallest mountain if you are climbing with the right people." There is no point in reaching for the top if the people around you are holding you back.

The people you hang out with are not just a reflection of your thinking and mindset; they are contributing to it. The person you associate with and spend the most time with measures your success.

When it comes to reaching your goals and objectives, the people you are in direct contact with will either help you get there, or hold you back. So choose wisely when you build your team. They are your warriors on this journey. You will need them when the going gets tough.

This is why, when taking on challenges that scare you, it is easier to go through the experience surrounded by people who are doing it too. Wouldn't you rather spend time with someone who is encouraging you to take action, rather than someone who habitually procrastinates?

Scared people who stay scared rarely do anything to change. They are too afraid to. And, the people who hang around with them often share a similar mindset. If you want to win, you have to stick with the people who are winning.

Four Strategies for Building Better Connections

1. Join a Mastermind Group

One of the best things I ever did was hook up with several mastermind groups online. Depending on what you are into, there are groups for just about any level of support these days. If you are finding it hard to partner up with the right people in your area, start with some online connections. It isn't the same as meeting up with someone for coffee, but you can chat in real-time and join live webinars.

A mastermind group is made up of people with similar interests. You can work toward goals, key objectives, and even start a business with online connections.

Nobody can make it alone. We need support, encouragement, and positive interaction with good people. Better yet, you can do things you'd normally put off with someone else. It is always easier if you are in the company of friends.

People partner up to take on projects, create businesses, or work on new innovations together. A solid partnership can make the difference between **doing it NOW**, and not doing it at all.

In the last ten years, social media has provided us with relationships that span the globe. We can connect through chats, video, or audio. There are very few boundaries these days. It is amazing. While we shouldn't rely entirely on online friends for support, there are times when we have to connect with people, the right people, wherever they may be. This is, in fact, how I continue to build my online platform.

2. Avoid the Scared People Who Spread Fear

We can find the people who support our mission by, first of all, letting go of the people who don't. Before we set out to find these people, we should take a look at the crowd in our lives and ask: *Will these people work with or against me? Are we working towards a common goal, or not?*

A friend of mine, who realized his dream after working in the wrong profession for nearly ten years, had surrounded himself with people who didn't support his goals. After carefully analyzing the situation, he gradually let people go by reducing the amount of time he spent with each of them. When he was ready to move on, nobody cared because he had created a totally new group of friends that shared a common interest in his new path.

People who live in fear and take no action will spread that fear to everyone they meet.

Their fear becomes a contagious virus and we should stay away from them. They'll eventually find their own crowd of haters.

What I've seen happen in several relationships is that the man or woman suddenly realizes they have a mission to fulfill. This could be a dream that must be recognized, a life purpose discovered, or something even greater.

As they become aware and try to share this newfound discovery with their partners, they are met with disappointment and resistance. The partner or spouse has a different agenda and isn't interested in the other person's new way of life.

I am not suggesting you walk away from all your relationships to live the life you've always dreamed of, but in many cases, this is what happens. We try to involve those in our lives at that time, but sometimes we come to realize, it's like trying to fit a round peg into a square hole. I've seen others do the opposite as well where instead of breaking free, they opt in to stick with their crowd and stay scared like the rest of them.

If you are partnered up with someone in your professional or personal life whose relationship is causing pain and stress, consider your options. Look for an exit strategy. Get out. Make it your mission to find the right crowd of people, because they are out there. But you'll struggle to connect with them if your mind set is elsewhere.

The scope of this book doesn't include walking you through major relationship shifts, but if you recognize your situation needs to be changed, you'll be the one to change it. Don't let toxicity ruin your chances of living a remarkable life. The wrong people can hold you back from your journey. The right people will help you get there.

3. Stick with Your Influencers

The people in your life not only influence your actions, but also your state of mind and attitude. The people you are with feed directly into your emotions. They impact your thoughts and affect motivation.

What you feel is how you act. If you are charged up emotionally and surrounded by positive people, there is no limit to what you can do. But hang with the naysayers who don't believe you can do it, tell you you're crazy or that what you are planning is impossible, and you'll start to act like it.

Connect with people who exchange ideas and are in it with you to further the quality of both your lives. If you can only connect with people online, that is better than hanging out in person with naysayers. Foster positive relationships and you'll reduce your scared factor exponentially. But stay connected to those negative relationships and you'll be afraid every waking moment.

Is there someone holding you back? Do you already have a supportive community helping you? Are you still unsure the type of crowd you need? Regardless of your situation, our goal is to create a positive community of friends, family members, and partners who can share insight, ideas and a common vision. If the right people are with you for the journey, they'll stick with you to the end.

4. Go Where Your Crowd Is

In order to discover your tribe, you have to know where they hang out and start hanging out there. **Focus** is key. Know who matters and whom you need to keep at a distance.

Emotionally disconnect from the people that are filling your mind with self-doubt. This can be tough to do if they are coworkers or family, but when we listen to the naysayers, we become one of them. It will happen without you being aware of it.

Remember that we become the model of those people in our lives. If you're not helping each other, you're most likely tearing each other and everyone else down. Know who you should focus on, and give that group or person your attention. You might be in a situation at work where you have to spend eight hours a day with people you don't like.

If this is the case, and because most people don't get to choose their coworkers, being around people you have negative feelings towards affects your mental health. It can be exhausting. You are always on guard.

A friend of mine recently went through a rough divorce after 15 years of marriage. When I asked him why he married in the first place, he said that in the beginning the relationship was a positive and healthy partnership. He felt energized by his partner, as if they were unbeatable. But, over the years, those feelings changed.

When the marriage turned toxic, and those positive emotions were replaced by contempt and negativity, it was time to get out. Eventually he separated and several years later he discovered the person of his dreams. He went on to build a successful business and turned what could have been an unhappy life into a positive event.

Without a doubt, the relationships you forge do matter.

A good relationship will make you; a bad one will break you. When you are showing up every day and the people around you are creating a fear-based, paralyzing environment, you have to change it, put up with it, or become a victim of circumstances.

Key Takeaways

- Find people who support, encourage, and believe in you. Reduce the amount of time and increase the amount of distance between you and the people who steal your energy. Naysayers are not welcome.
- Identify the relationships in your life that do you harm. These can be toxic and unhealthy to your success. Worse yet, they promote fear and are keeping you from acting. Then, look for ways to break away and reduce the amount of proximity time.
- Stay active and hook up with the right people. They are out there, but you'll have to find them. Know the kind of people you want to forge partnerships with. Follow them online, send them messages, or

make plans to meet. Model what they are doing and ask lots of questions.

- Emulate the kind of success you want and hang out with the right people who are committed to continuous support and encouragement.

At the Risk of
Looking Stupid

"Fearlessness is not only possible, it is the ultimate joy. When you touch nonfear, you are free."

— Thich Nhat Hanh

The #1 obstacle that stands between us and doing it scared is the fear of failing and looking like a fool.

We all know that feeling. Everyone is watching you. Some are waiting for you to make a mistake or fail so they can make an example out of you. Now, your boss at work just handed you a project on a subject you know little about.

Your initial thoughts are:

What if I screw up? What if I look incompetent? I'll lose face in front of everyone and then I'll have to look for another job. But what if it happens again at the next job? When will I stop feeling this way?

The fear of taking action leads to inaction. The fear of looking stupid triggers avoidance mechanisms and you go into paralysis mode. You look for a way out, a way to escape. People who are afraid of looking dumb often judge others when they screw up.

Risk is an opportunity to fail. You avoid putting yourself out there because, somewhere along the way, you've adopted a set of limiting beliefs that are keeping you trapped. Risking anything by taking a chance on a new idea, venture, or relationship, feeds into our fear of rejection. People who are afraid of being rejected, and have instilled that fear as a kind of phobia, are masters of avoiding risky situations.

Here are some examples:

- You don't ask someone out because you think they'll say NO and you'll look like a fool.
- You don't apply for that job you want because you think there will be tons of applicants and you'll look stupid going up against such tough competition.
- You don't start that book because you think you suck as a writer. So why humiliate yourself by having people read your bad writing?
- You don't voice your opinion during a conversation because you think you might say the wrong thing and, once again, sound like an idiot.

It's true that there is risk in taking chances. People who are overly sensitive and shy will be affected more than those that charge full speed ahead. The difference is, those charging ahead are probably afraid too, but they are willing to take a chance to find what lies beyond their fear.

This is a powerful lesson we can learn from. We spend so much time and effort avoiding what we are scared of because we don't want to face the humiliation of making a mistake. But, when we don't put ourselves out there, we make no progress. We stay the same. We stay stuck.

In sixth grade, I was terrified of playing baseball. It is, perhaps, the only sport I can say I hate more than anything. I know, it is loved by millions of fans and one of the most popular sports in both the US and Japan, but when I was growing up, playing baseball was the same as looking like a complete fool. Here is why.

When I was up to bat, I would strike out nine times out of ten. Perfect pitches came across the plate and I would still miss the ball entirely. When I was in the outfield and the ball came my way, I'd fumble it almost every time.

I could neither catch nor hit. In other words, not only was I the worst player on the team, but also, I'd get taunted by the other players for never being able to hit or catch the ball.

Baseball just wasn't my sport. I developed a fear of playing because I was tired of looking stupid. The other players, even the ones on my own team, laughed whenever I stepped up to the plate, struck out, or missed a fly ball. It was embarrassing.

I learned to dislike the sport because it instilled in me a fear of looking dumb. It sapped my confidence, and I left my self-esteem at the plate every time.

There are many other examples of things I've failed at. My performance in school was weak, and most years I would barely scrape by with passing grades. Over time, I identified myself as someone who wasn't smart or successful. Gradually, I stopped taking risks or striving for what I wanted. My fear of failing had instilled in me a belief that it was better to not try and put myself on the spot than do it and end up looking bad.

Why Looking Stupid Is So Shameful

The alternative to doing it scared is living with shame. After a lifetime of failing or looking bad, we learn to cover up what we don't want the world to see. We all have weak spots, and to protect ourselves we hide these weaknesses from everyone, including ourselves.

We learn at a young age to avoid failing. Like not being able to hit a ball in the big game, we don't want to be singled out as the one who isn't going to make it. So instead we try to blend in, play by the rules, and do just enough to not get noticed for playing bad or well.

You want to ask someone out on a date, but if he or she says no, you are left with that feeling of rejection and it validates your sense of low esteem. So we avoid the risks and stay below the radar. But that is not the place success thrives.

We can only be confident when we act with confidence, regardless of the outcome. When I was trying to hit a ball and I couldn't, it didn't matter. I was at the plate and trying to smash a home run. When others laughed, it didn't matter because with every swing, I got closer to that big play.

Just as in baseball, in life you need to step up to the plate and take your turn at bat. If you strike out, it doesn't mean you'll fail at everything. But you will if you say no to everything. It's okay to miss your shot, whether it be in sports or failing a job interview.

Becoming Fearless

Gary Vaynerchuck is one of my favorite speakers. As the founder of the #AskGaryVee Show, he is a prolific entrepreneur, author, and Internet personality.

But what I like most about him is his fearlessness. Gary tells it how it is and he doesn't sugar coat anything.

Gary has delivered keynote speeches to millions of people. He is direct, straightforward, and honest. He shows us that we can do whatever we want to do if we can get over that fear of failing.

As Gary says:

"If I said one of the hardest things about making your dream, or your small business, or your blog, or whatever, happen was just *doing it*, would you believe me? Because the truth is, that *is* the hardest part. And ironically, that is the one big thing standing in your way. Just executing. Nobody can argue with execution. Once you're getting shit done, you're on your way."

You might be scared, putting it off, avoiding what needs to be done, but once you do something, you're triggered to charge forward. You become fearless by pushing through the fear and doing what scares you. If you're waiting for permission to take action, give yourself permission. Be fearless by looking at your fear through the other end of the scope.

Think of it this way. You're going to die someday. Do you want to look back with regret on the things you ran away from? Do you want to be one of those people who dies knowing you could have been larger than life and serving a life greater than your own? You have this life to charge forward and do your thing.

How to Evaluate a Win-Win Situation

Where would you be without mistakes? Can you remember the last time you made a big mistake? How did you feel or react? Did you take responsibility?

I once worked with someone who blamed all his mistakes on everyone else. No matter what happened, it was someone else's fault, even when it clearly wasn't. This person also lived with a lot of fear, pointing his finger or denying that he'd done anything wrong at all. He was so scared of the world that he never interacted with others or made friends, either at work or outside of it.

This person was always on edge, looking out for himself, never trying anything different or challenging because he feared screwing it up. When the company shifted gears and needed people who could think innovatively, he didn't make the team. The world needs more people who are ready to take action when scared and not run away from fear.

But fear affects all of us differently. You could be a perfectly rational human being and then, when put into a situation that threatens your security, start to lie, cheat, and act in a way that suggests you've been taken over by aliens.

A mentor of mine used a unique approach. He would look at each day as a new opportunity to grow, do something different, and embrace the time he had. He was honest and laughed at his own mistakes, and he made more mistakes than anyone. Why? Because he tried so many new things. It didn't matter if it was related to a tech issue he knew nothing about, or taking on a new role he wasn't prepared for.

When a challenge presented itself, he would take it. When he wasn't asked, he volunteered. You see, many people avoid being selected for new things. They would rather hide in the shadows and hope that somebody else gets picked. But that's not how we get better.

What stops many people from taking action is the fear of losing what they have. But what do we really have if what we hold isn't what we want? How can we call ourselves wealthy when we live in fear of scarcity? What will happen if you take that risk and succeed?

The fear of looking like a fool is related to low self-esteem and perfectionism. You are worried about what the people will think. Great achievements are made when people put themselves out there and take chances. By not doing anything, you are denying yourself the opportunity to be great. You don't want to be great? You're not reading this book because you love mediocrity.

You believe in the possibility that you can cultivate a life that is more than just ordinary. There is nothing wrong with ordinary either, but let's face it, who doesn't want to do something extraordinary at least once in their lives?

We all have a gift and ability to do something brilliant with our lives. Find out what it is and make it happen.

Key Takeaways

- Reflect on a time when you did something without worrying about looking foolish [this should be when you were not intoxicated]. What was the result?
- Make a list of things you avoid because you fear looking foolish. It could be that you're scared of failing in front of a group, or, looking silly just isn't your thing.
- Record a video of yourself speaking to your audience. This can be anything. You can record yourself trying to do 50 pushups every day or twenty minutes of resistance training. People love it when you share the greatest parts of yourself. You can record it and then, when you are feeling more confident, you can start up a Facebook group or YouTube channel.

Disguising Fear with Distraction

"All the adversity I've had in my life, all my troubles and obstacles, have strengthened me... You may not realize it when it happens, but a kick in the teeth may be the best thing in the world for you."

— Walt Disney

Since the Internet has radically shaped the way we live — bringing access to social media, games, and unlimited information — this generation has been accused of creating a world of productivity killing distractions. When I don't feel like doing something, I find a way to escape it.

In today's world, this is easy to do. There is no limit to the number of distractions we can use to keep our minds fixed on something else. The problem is, these distractions are set up to lead us away from working on the tasks and goals that matter.

Here is an example: you have a project that needs to be finished in three days and you've hit a rough spot. Instead of digging in and fixing the problem, you start a new project, or change gears and begin doing something completely unrelated to get your mind off of it.

You promise to get back to it first thing the next morning. But the next day you are busy doing something else. You keep finding reasons why it can't be done. Then Friday comes, you've missed the deadline, and you lose the contract with the customer.

Sounds familiar? It's happened to all of us. For some people, it has turned into an addiction. Think back to a time when you put something off because the thought of doing it created so much resistance that you couldn't deal with. This can be anything, but our need to be distracted is merely an excuse generator. You might feel busy, but are you really? Is what you are doing right now more important than what you know needs to be done?

Creating distractions has never been easier than it is in today's world. We are always just an arm's reach away from a device or remote control. We can access whatever we desire any time of the day. In other words, we are living limitless in a world with unlimited choices to keep our minds as busy [and distracted] as possible.

We all struggle with 'distraction obstacles.' Whenever I come across a problem that is challenging and that I'd rather not tackle, my first instinct is to find something else to do to divert my attention from the problem. This is what I refer to as *fear avoidance*. We avoid dealing with difficult issues by replacing them with something that is fun and easier to deal with. This is how procrastination happens.

When we avoid tough situations, like paying bills or having difficult conversations with people, we are putting off an inevitable fearful situation that isn't going to go away. As soon as we think *I can't handle this*, we'll do anything to avoid it. But what we turn a blind eye towards doesn't just disappear. Unresolved situations are stressful, and we carry the internal stress around with us wherever we go.

When situations or difficulties are unresolved, you become exhausted quicker. Your mind is working overtime to figure out a solution while you are busy trying to keep it distracted. Until we can deal with the problem and reach a resolution, we will always feel the burden of the things that are left incomplete.

Here are a few examples of tough situations that, when avoided, trigger stress:

- Unpaid bills that cause creditors to call your home.
- Avoiding a conversation with someone that leads to a misunderstanding and worsens the situation.
- Putting off finding a new job leads you to have to do more work you hate.
- Eating junk food instead of a healthy meal leads to bigger health problems and weight gain.
- Rapid life changes that disrupts the normal flow of your routine.

I get the whole *I'll take care of it later* routine. For years, I avoided every uncomfortable situation. I became a passive observer in life, and it led to more problems than I can count. Issues went unresolved, resentments built-up and turned relationships sour, and my unhappiness hit an all-time low. It became obvious to me that fear avoidance is a short-term plan that sets us up to fail.

You might escape the problem in the NOW, but you'll pay for it LATER. When we put off tasks and projects that we should do NOW, and replace them with passive activities such as watching TV or surfing the Internet without any purpose other than to kill time, we're creating bad habits that can spiral out of control.

Procrastination and the Art of Postponing Critical Work

From a young age, I learned to procrastinate and put everything off. But *later* wasn't that far in the future. In school I put off doing homework until the last minute only to rush through it when it had to be done. For years, I put off creating a financial plan only to be hit with large credit card bills and bankruptcy.

Over the course of time, I had developed the habit of saying I would *do it later*. When you buy into short-term pleasure, you are investing in long-term pain. What you focus on is eventually what you become.

Buying into short-term pleasure is investing in long-term pain. *This is the core of our fear.*

It wasn't until years later that I learned to confront my fear. When I was scared, I moved forward with a plan of action. Even a simple plan is better than nothing. The act of running away was so ingrained that it became an automatic response. If you want more freedom in your life, you need to take care of business — unfinished business.

Time management creator and productivity consultant **David Allen** calls this "Getting Things Done." This is exactly what we need to shift towards: getting the things that scare us the most finished. It is these obstacles we face every day that are the hardest to maneuver around.

What I propose is this: make a list of the stuff you have been avoiding. Do it now.

For example, here is a short list of what I have been avoiding:

- Talking with my wife about money issues.
- Hiring someone to design my website so I can run my online business.
- De-cluttering the house so we have more room to breathe.
- Talking with a co-worker about their unacceptable behavior.
- Starting a report that has to be finished in two days.
- Cancelling my credit card.
- Making a dental appointment.

By the time I had finished my list there were over forty things I'd been avoiding. By avoiding what needed to be done, I created a stressful lifestyle. It's like a garbage heap you keep throwing trash onto and then when it's huge, you try to cover it up. It stinks after a while until you find a new place to move it. So, get in the habit of clearing away your junk pile. Don't let it stink.

I've learned that when I trained myself, through positive habit development, to take care of business right away, I felt empowered. With everything I had to do, I was overwhelmed and took no action at all. I would always say, *I'll do it tomorrow.* Tomorrow would come and I'd get busy with something else. By keeping myself occupied with other things, I avoided doing the stuff that mattered most.

You might be forced into doing it scared, but that's nothing like the fear you'll have years later when you start to pay for the consequences of your procrastination. Do you want to pay now or later? Do you want to suffer now or even worse later? Do you want to go through a difficult period now or later?

Do it now, get the things that are holding you back done, and push through the challenges that are in your way. Start now by taking action on the one thing that scares you.

Here is a short list of the **distractors** that keep you **scared**. Can you add any more to this list?

- TV [when it is used to numb out and escape]
- Addictions
- Entertainment sources that keep us busy
- Harmful relationships

- Overeating
- Compulsive shopping
- Excessive social media interaction
- Compulsive email and texting

We can use anything to distract ourselves from the fear of reality, but is it reality or the illusion that is more frightening? Reality can be terrifying, and the world is not at a loss for activities that divert our attention when we need it.

Getting Connected with Reality

I know someone who watched TV for a month because he was afraid to deal with a painful divorce. He said that when he watched television it was like he became a device that tuned everything else out. But, when the distraction was gone, the pain returned. And, it would come back with nasty ferocity. There is nothing wrong with watching some TV, but when you over-use things as a means to escape you are setting yourself up to fail in the long term.

I know what it's like to be stuck in a situation that is terrifying to deal with. We all deal with fear differently. Going through a bad relationship, sickness, bankruptcy, or even dealing with day-to-day living can be stressful.

Remember that everything is temporary. It passes. You can get through it no matter what. The time will pass regardless, and if you decide to confront your difficulties now instead of avoiding them you'll be able to enjoy yourself later, which has so much more to offer.

When we lose the ability to cope, we distract ourselves with actions that disable our power. The things we try to avoid don't just disappear. As many recovering alcoholics have discovered when they first became sober, life is always happening even when they aren't present. The problems they avoided were usually left unattended and either became worse or, someone else had to step in and take care of it.

When we turn away from fear, we are making a conscious decision not to handle it. We are, in fact, saying no to becoming great.

When we run we make life more difficult than it has to be. Or worse, we admit that we can't handle it, and it is better left unresolved. Or, we hope that someone else steps in to do something.

As I said earlier in this book, we make two choices at the beginning of each day: either we empower ourselves to take action or, we live scared by running away from our problems and stay in hiding.

Make a choice and take a stand right now to stop running and start doing. Tackle your actions with intention.

When we take on challenges that frighten us, it increases our ability to handle any situation. We never have the chance to learn from what we avoid and run from. It's like shooting yourself in the foot. You might con yourself into thinking you're getting away with it, but this is a lie you shouldn't believe.

Reality can be frightening, but as I learned the hard way, not nearly as frightening as waking up one day and realizing you can no longer turn off the problem. You need to either fight or fail. There can be no victory when the challenges we face defeat us. You are only defeated if you make up your mind to be. It's never over until you've given up.

Key Takeaways

- Stay focused when you feel like running. Stand your ground and ask yourself: *what am I risking by not standing up to this situation?*
- Be aware of your distractors. We all have our favorite devices. Catch yourself when you are using something to zone out or escape. This is a sign you are practicing fear avoidance.
- Make a list of the things that distract you and reinforce the action habit: **Take action with intention.** Don't wait. The longer you wait, the more difficult it will be to solve the problem later. Do you want to suffer now or later? Short-term pain leads to long-term happiness.
- Everything is temporary. When we avoid the things that must be done, we are just inviting more stress into our lives. Unfinished business remains that way until you take responsibility for it.

Putting Your Self-Doubt
on the Ropes

Self-doubt is a very powerful form of fear. Robbing people of confidence, self-esteem, and creating deep-seated hopelessness, it is the #1 dream killer.

Self-doubt kills motivation and causes you to hesitate to take action. Not knowing what to do next, you become paralyzed with fear that keeps you stuck in the same repetitive cycle, even if the cycle isn't working.

Let's get focused on how to eliminate self-doubt and improve your game in life.

Why Do We Doubt Ourselves?

We all have stories of losing confidence and failing to follow through when we were scared or didn't want to deal with a situation. In times of deep fear, it's in our nature to defend ourselves, to flee and protect our fragile ego.

Many people have suffered from self-doubt for so long and from such a young age that they don't know any other way to live. In severe cases, some of us turn to introversion or build fantasies around how life should be instead of how it is.

To change, we have to stay grounded in the reality of what is happening now. But there are no shortcuts to overcoming feelings of self-doubt. It is a decision you need to make each day.

For today, you will take at least one progressive action to raise your confidence level. You will reach out to people who need help, and you will ask for help in return. You could do one thing you are resisting. You could throw out your negative thoughts and replace them with positive affirmations.

You can turn introversion and fear into extroversion and courage. It all starts with a simple action. You could implement a positive thought that pushes you to overcome a limiting belief. Or, when you are retreating into yourself and the voices of doubt fill your mind, you can recognize what is happening and try to correct it.

The key to taking control of your life is deciding what you are willing to accept and what you are not willing to accept. I, for example, refuse to allow the voices that occupy my mind to control my thoughts. If they control my thoughts, they tap into my fear. When that happens, fear takes over and I fall back into a mental prison again.

When you choose to take the *Nothing Scares Me* approach, you are holding the key to your freedom. Now you can turn the key and do something about it.

The Beliefs that Create Doubt

In the beginning of this book I told you I failed throughout most of my school years. The main reason, I realized later, was because I had built up a powerful resistance to failing. Instead of taking on new challenges, I avoided them. I distracted myself, filling my valuable time with activities I couldn't fail at: video games, television, or playing around with social media [you know, cat videos].

What is the problem with this? When you repeatedly practice habits that lead you away from your true objectives, they become your default strategy whenever *scared* moments appear.

By creating a predictable lifestyle in your comfort zone, you strengthen the walls of your mental and emotional prison. Your comfort zone is not always a bad place, but the more you stay there the less you progress.

Self-doubt is like fungus in the mind; it needs a place to grow. Unknowingly and subconsciously, many people feed into their self-doubt every minute of the day with addictions, limiting beliefs, worn-out thoughts, and out-of-control behaviors that destroy character.

When we overcome, we become greater. When we run, we are reduced to mediocre shadows of what we could be.

The First Instinct

Every moment that challenges you and every new problem you experience will scare you. That's it. With every situation, I have ever faced, from getting on an airplane for the first time, moving to a new country, starting at a new company, or meeting new people, anxiety and fear are all part of the game.

You might think there is something wrong with you if you feel afraid to give a speech, but this is perfectly normal. In fact, it is necessary. When you **take massive action** in the face of fear, you improve your game. By doing something new, you become stronger. By taking action, you build your confidence and eliminate self-doubt.

Controlling Your Fear

Several years ago I attended a conference to listen to several keynote speakers. For the record, public speaking is a terrifying experience that I struggle to overcome even today.

At this conference the speaker, who had just finished giving a speech to over one hundred people, suddenly handed the podium over to me. A minute before I had been enjoying sitting at a table, watching, and listening. There was no pressure to do anything. Suddenly, I was being asked to deliver some words to this large group without any preparation.

My first initial reaction was to leave. I wanted to run. If I had been sitting near an emergency exit I might have. I broke out in sweat. It was cold fear, and I was stuck in a spot I couldn't get out of. My colleague was holding out the mic and it took me several seconds to realize I wasn't reaching for it. Then in the process of taking it I stood up and nearly fell over. Rubbery legs. Dry throat. I knew that I had to deliver and that there was no running away. My self-doubt screamed, *this is it! You're going to crash and burn!*

I successfully delivered a short speech without panicking. I knew, in that moment, that this was how you get over the fear of doing anything: by doing it. I just relaxed and spoke as if I was speaking to an audience of friends. If I started to think about my words, or doubt that what I was saying was worthy, the panic would creep in. Leaving perfection out of the equation is what pulled me through.

This simple practice can work for you too. We get focused on doing it right or we doubt that we aren't good enough. You might think, "If only I have another day to practice this it'll be much better." What we are doing is putting it off. This creates more anxiety. The longer you take to think it over and consider if your actions are right, the more opportunity you are giving yourself to screw it up. By the time it's game time, you are shaking so bad you'd rather be anyplace else.

You can only win the game by playing the game. The next time somebody challenges you to take action and step outside your comfort zone, accept it and thank that person right away.

I learned something powerful in those moments of fear: it can be controlled.

This is how you deal with those scared moments. You face the truth that this challenge is not a punishment, but something that will make you better, develop your character, and push you out of the comfort zone. Remember that, as you reach out and try new things, you'll always be afraid. But that scared moment is temporary. Fear doesn't last forever. You can, however, spend the rest of your life regretting the things you don't do.

Mastering Your Mind

One of the most powerful weapons you have is the mastery of your mind. Self-doubt is like an illness that attempts to rob you of this mastery. It makes you weaker by feeding into your fears.

And what do we fear most?

Confronting problems, new experiences, and the fear of failing. You are going to challenge the self-doubt in your life by challenging the negative voices in your head, the thoughts you create, and the anxiety feeding off your fearful state. This sounds like a lot to take in, but it is a formula that works.

As we question our fears, we can see the lies that exist. Self-doubt is created when our fears are made real. When we fail, it feeds our fears, but only if we believe failure is a bad thing, only when we judge ourselves too harshly or believe that all is lost. You stay scared when you think there is no way out. If you stay trapped behind closed doors, you'll never break free.

Are you ready to open those doors?

Tactics for Challenging Your Self-Doubt

I use a simple formula to challenge my fears and doubt. I know it works because I've been using it for years when I am faced with difficulty, challenges, and problems.

Challenge #1: You Will Always Have Self-doubt Until You Do Something. You can't just *think* yourself into a successful outcome. You have to take action and do the thing you're afraid of. Self-doubt, fear, and uncertainty are facts of life. We all have fears until we rise above the challenge. Take action when you're feeling self-doubt and you'll crush it every time. Avoid and run away and the doubt will stick around.

Action is powerful. It puts you in control of the situation instead of becoming a victim of circumstances. Taking action instantly boosts your confidence. It is the one solution that never fails. Provided, of course, that you are taking the right actions and doing something that brings you closer to your goals. This is the first step in creating that thriving lifestyle you are after.

The question is, what are you going to do today? Right now, write down [in pen and on paper] one action that you will take today to push back against your doubts. This can involve a current challenge you are facing, or something you've been putting off because you fear failing.

We all have these so it should be easy to choose something.

Challenge #2: Everyone Is Scared. We see people as superhuman when they get out there and do what seems impossible. But what appears impossible to many is simply an obstacle to some. Any obstacle can be removed when you decide to confront life's difficulties.

Do you think you are the only one who's scared? Is fear and self-doubt exclusive to your life? No, we all have it. Your case isn't any more special than mine. What differentiates us is how we control our fear and do what scares us even when our instincts tell us to give up.

We're all scared. But this can be used to our advantage. If you want to master your life, do the one thing that scares you the most.

Make a list of the things you are scared of. There is no shame in this. Creating the list will bring the stuff you should be aware of to light. Awareness of our fear is the first step to removing it. Make your list right now.

Challenge #3: Forge a Confident Identity. Convert your identity from someone who believes they are a failure to someone who is a true winner. Deep feelings of doubt and uncertainty can mold themselves into an identity. That is to say, we identify ourselves as people who lack confidence.

Have you ever said to someone, "I'm not a confident person"? In saying that, you act it out. Our words have power. Repeating is the same as molding ourselves into that image.

You were not born with doubt; you created it. Recognizing this helps you shift from a victim to someone who can handle anything. If you identify yourself as someone who is afraid to fail, you'll continue to fail. If you label yourself as weak or incapable of handling fearful situations, then you'll run every time something happens. By shifting your identity, you can gain greater personal power.

Self-doubt is only as strong as the power you feed it. Take away its power with positive self-talk. Replace your negative voice with powerful choice words. When you experience doubt, ask yourself: "What am I thinking or doing that makes me feel this way? How can I shift away from this thought?" By questioning the power it has on you, you take away its power and give yourself greater confidence to step up to a new level.

Avoid saying things like:

- I'm no good at this.
- I don't have the confidence to succeed.
- I don't want to fail so why bother.
- Who am I to try this?
- I don't have the talent or creativity.

Stay focused on every word spoken. What you say and how you say it fuels your desire to take action. Your words create concrete thoughts and beliefs. Your thoughts control your words and manage your confidence. Stay focused on your thoughts above all else.

Key Takeaways

- When you repeatedly practice habits that lead you away from your true objectives, they become your default strategy whenever *scared* moments appear.
- Self-doubt is the negative belief that you are incompetent, incapable, and seemingly hopelessly unable to succeed. Do you think so? Is this true? Or are you being manipulated by a lower state of mind? Is your doubt in your own character a permanent flaw, or do you believe it can be turned around?
- Everyone is scared. We all have doubts and uncertainties. What matters is how we confront these fears.
- Listen to your negative voices. What are they telling you? Do you believe the thoughts that you are creating? Focus on this self-talk and learn to talk back.
- Negative internal dialogue is your fear taking over. Create your own dialogue by turning off the negativity and replacing it with powerful words that build up your confidence.

Breaking Bad Habits That Keep You Scared

"It is easier to prevent bad habits than to break them."

— Benjamin Franklyn

Your habits play an important role in your success. We already know this, but the challenge comes in knowing which habits are good and which damage our lifestyle. Habits aren't good or bad unless they hold you back from achieving what you truly desire in your life.

If you want better health, obviously eating excessive amounts of junk food or smoking would be categorized as bad habits. Charles Duhigg, bestselling author of *The Power of Habit*, said: *The Golden Rule of Habit Change: You can't extinguish a bad habit, you can only change it.*

If we can't discern the good from the bad, we end up taking actions without thinking about what we are working for. When you climb the wrong ladder, it doesn't matter if you reach the top or not. This same principal applies to building better habits to put us on a more focused path.

In my years of experience, I have seen people continue to perform poorly, not from lack of skill or knowledge, but because they had poor habits that set them up for failure.

The problem is that we don't know what we don't know, and when it comes to habit formation, we don't know which habits are helping us and which are hurting us. Even sometimes when it feels like we are doing the right thing, that habit can be hurting our chances of getting ahead.

Our passive habits make us afraid to take action. These habits are automatic, and we feed them repeatedly throughout the day without any conscious effort. Passive habits may include:

- Sleeping in late because that is what you have always done.
- Spending money you don't have when you're bored.
- Watching TV for hours to avoid working.
- Scrolling through social media feeds looking for something interesting to entertain you.
- Eating junk food without any thought to how we will feel the next day.

Implementing Good Habits

For years, my habits kept me scared. We all have habits that we want to change, but without knowing what changes we want, creating better habits becomes more difficult. When you successfully change a habit, you aren't only making a shift in your actions, but also in your emotions. Adjusting the related habits can lead to a major shift in your emotions.

But, what exactly is a good habit? How do we define a bad one? Obviously, smoking is a bad habit due to the health risks, but to the person who smokes, the habit itself provides a sense of relief. They have formed an emotional trigger with the habit that signifies pleasure, relief, and the temporary removal of stress.

Here is an example of a good habit I have implemented: I write 2,000 words every morning for my blog and books. Because I implemented this habit, I have been able to produce over 40 blog posts this year and written seven books in the past eighteen months. With the development and consistent action of this one habit, I am now enjoying success as an author.

But it wasn't always this way.

For years, I spent my time watching TV and playing video games. I did everything except write, even though I had the desire to do it. But watching TV excessively or passing time with any other passive habit doesn't bring our dreams to life; it steals them away.

Bad habits were robbing me of what I really wanted. The only way to write my first book was to taper down my TV-watching time by 80 percent. I finally did this and got the work done. As a result, I felt more confident and that gave me the momentum I needed to work harder. This momentum led me to develop better habits in the morning and a stronger work ethic that changed my identity.

Just as practicing good habits can boost confidence, practicing destructive habits rob you of it. Here is an example:

Darie [a friend of mine] wants to lose weight. This has been her long-term goal for the past several years. She usually starts strong for the first month but loses interest and goes back to gorging.

When she was sticking to the diet, she lost several pounds but then returned to the damaging habit of eating crap again. Why? She felt great when she could see her progress, but, as everyone knows, it gets harder when you don't see expected results soon enough. Then we return to old ways of thinking and fall into comfortable routines so we will feel good about ourselves again.

Comfortable routines are predictable. We know what to expect from them. They rarely disappoint us because it is impossible to fail at them. But developing a new routine focused on a goal is a risk. We get scared of what could be and feel a strong pull to return to the predictability of a failed outcome.

What bad habits can you replace with good ones? What is it you hope to achieve with this new arrangement?

The Habits that Keep You Scared

For years, I had several habits that kept me scared and trapped. Procrastination was at the top of the list. I was always in the habit of neglecting what needed to be done. For example, creating a life plan, a financial plan, or mapping out my goals were all things I wanted to accomplish, but whenever I thought about them there was something more pressing to do.

Procrastination, while it felt like I was in control because I could make the decision to do or not do something, was robbing me of the life I could have had. The habit of doing it later became destructive. And, because I wasn't getting the things done that should have been, I was always scared of the future. Will I be okay? What if I run out of money? What is going to happen to my life?

When you develop the right habits, fear has no place in your life. To feel positive and enthusiastic about the future, we need structure and an organized plan, even if it is only a temporary one. Whenever I tried to act on my bad habits they would lead back to more procrastination. Then I'd experience a deep sense of fear that had returned. Bad habits are those that hold you back from achieving the impossible. You'll never be great with mediocre habits.

Right now, identify three bad habits you'd like to kick. Once identified, ask yourself: *why is it important for me to replace these habits with something else?* Without a strong enough answer, chances are you'll struggle to succeed at replacing them and eventually slip back into old routines, do what you've always done, and get what you've always gotten.

Five Steps for Breaking Bad Habits

Step 1: Recognize the Routine

Every habit has a place of origin. It thrives in a certain environment triggered by a stimulus. The routine is your way of feeding the habit. We give it what it desires the most: a reward. By feeding bad habits they are able to stay strong and control you.

A routine is a set of actions repeated consistently, often subconsciously. It is triggered by an external or internal stimulus in which we feel the need to feed this habit by giving into the impulse.

For most people, it is an addiction of some sort, such as smoking, checking email often, or compulsively shopping. Once you decide the course of action, it follows a set pattern and, if there is an emotional reward, you will continue to repeat the behavior.

Once you recognize the routine of your habit, you can implement a new set of actions to change it.

Step 2: Identify the Trigger

This is the point where we can catch our bad habit as it is stimulated by a trigger. This can be anything from an environmental trigger, watching something on TV, a feeling we suddenly get, or a certain person we meet.

The trigger, in this case, is the key. Once you identify what triggers you to take action, this is the point you are going to make a decision to either act...or not.

Your trigger is often an impulsive act. We don't think but react when it is switched on. It's purely compulsive. Addictions are formed through triggers. When we can recognize the trigger approaching, such as a craving for doing something, it becomes easier to turn it around.

Step 3: Replace the Action and Create New Behavior

If you make the conscious choice to not act when the trigger is activated, you have to replace the intended action [how you would normally react] with a new action. This new pattern, if repeated and implementing the replacement action, will form the new habit over a matter of weeks or months.

Just using willpower alone to try and not act out isn't enough. If you bare-knuckle it, you'll never recover. This is like an addict trying to kick the habit cold turkey without making attempts to replace the addiction. We need to know what the routine is, and then, when we are triggered to respond, be ready to take a different set of actions that break the habit.

For example: You might be triggered to buy something online because you are bored. How can you replace this? Step away from the computer as soon as the trigger hits you. Get busy with another activity. You could even shut down your computer for the night and do something else that will break the impulse.

Step 4: Focus on Small, Incremental Changes

Reframing a habit takes time. You won't reinvent all your habits right away, but you will if you repeatedly switch your triggers and make yourself aware of the areas in which you are weak.

If your habit is wasting time on social media when you could be doing more constructive things, create a plan and a system to move away from this habit. With so many distractions, wasting time on worthless activities is common.

The changes may be small, but any shift in your attitude, emotions, or actions is going to have a long-term impact if practiced consistently. This is how habits are formed, and this is how they can be reinvented.

Step 5: Focus on Your New Reward

There has to be a driving force behind change. Otherwise, what is the point? Earlier we talked about the Ostrich Approach and how we bury our heads in the sand to escape reality. This escape tactic is, in many ways, a reward for people.

We can avoid the current reality that is frightening, and live as if everything is just fine. But when we get real about what is actually happening in our lives and make changes, the rewards are revealed much later.

In the immediate gratification approach, you might feel good now because you're seemingly getting away with: paying your bills, having a discussion, or accepting an illness. But, the immediate gratification approach has poor long-term rewards. In the end, you end up losing more than if you had taken action in the beginning.

To change a habit, you have to see the reward that is to come, but it might take months or years before you see any results. That's okay. If it were easy, everyone would be doing it.

Think of it this way: even though you might be scared to set up a financial plan for yourself, ten years from now, your family will be so much better off if you start today. Always have the reward serve as a reminder of what is yet to come. Don't let it go. Keep it there in the front of your mind at all times.

Key Takeaways

Create a Nothing Scares Me Journal: *A System for Recording Your Victories.*

You can monitor your habit changing progress. Do this whenever a trigger moment occurs – when you are bored or meet someone that makes you want to react a certain way.

By not giving into this feeling, you have just gained points. Every time you say NO, it paves the way for a larger YES down the road.

When you create a journal, dedicate a section or page to one habit you are working on reinventing. Record your progress, changes made, and most of all, how you really feel about committing to this habit changing challenge.

Failing at What You Love to Do Best

"I can accept failure, everyone fails at something. But I can't accept not trying."

— Michael Jordan

There is a myth that people who successfully live a life of passion and do what they love, were born with some innate skill. We are disillusioned in thinking that the reason we are not yet successful is, merely, because we don't have what it takes, or that we were not born with the same talents.

You might catch yourself saying things like, *wow, she's lucky* or, *that guy has got to be some kind of creative genius.*

I have met many creative people in my life. They do have talent, skill, and a drive I admire. But they weren't necessarily born with it. It is a skill that has been practiced with love and persistence.

When you love what you do you will do anything to become good at it. Born a genius or not, every master has to practice what they love to do, even when they don't want to.

We hear success stories of online entrepreneurs who've created the next Facebook or revolutionary product, or of unknown authors suddenly striking it big with bestsellers they wrote overnight. No matter the field, I don't believe anybody is brilliant or lucky enough that they can just show up, perform, and get paid millions. It does happen on occasion, but for the majority of those who succeed at doing what they love, it is a combination of passion, perseverance, and organized planning.

What we may perceive as luck or talent is, hidden behind the curtain, a lot of hard work and drive. You *drive* forward in what you love, and push hard to master it.

What are you driving for right now? What pushes you through to do what you love? If you know the answer to this, you're a huge step ahead. When you do what you love and you work at it every day, you are building a platform for success. This may take one year, or it may take twenty.

We have to take action and do what scares us most so we can live our lives as thriving examples of our own unique genius. We can do this by doing what we love, and by doing it poorly at first. When you successfully fail at what you love most, but continue to work and fail no matter how many attempts you make, then you've tapped into the secret formula.

The people who succeed at doing what they love will do what they have to do in order to master their passion, even when they don't feel like doing it. Taking action when you feel motivated isn't good enough. Motivation isn't always consistent. There is a deeper element in play that I call the *fear of regret*.

The Fear of Failing

We all have at least one regret. The things we wish we had done. The things we wish we'd said. But regret is grounded in the past. It ties you to a series of failed outcomes. This kills your confidence and drags down your self-esteem.

Self-esteem is something we need a lot of. If you are constantly focused on what could have been, it is impossible to focus on what could be. We should never trade in old memories for the chance to create new ones. In other words, we can create our future without repeating the same mistakes of the past.

Our motivation comes from focusing on what could be. It comes from the possibility of living your thriving lifestyle tomorrow, and not from the life you could have had. Abandon those thoughts that tie you to something that *can never be*. Get into the headspace of *what will be*.

Have you heard about Michael Jordan's practice sessions and the discipline he put into becoming the best basketball player on the planet?

Michael Jordan was cut from the high school basketball tryouts and told he'd never make it as a player. But he had grit, discipline, and a love for the game. Michael

Jordan would show up hours before the game and practice hundreds of shots. Michael failed over and over. But his missed shots were necessary to push him to practice and carry his career to the top, helping him win the Most Valuable Player Award five times and lead the Bulls to six NBA championships.

> *"I've missed more than 9,000 shots in my career. I've lost almost 300 games. Twenty-six times, I've been trusted to take the game winning shot and missed. I've failed over and over and over again in my life. And that is why I succeed."*

> **— Michael Jordan**

Another example is 'master of horror' author **Stephen King**, who has written over 60 international bestselling novels to earn the *Bram Stoker Award* and *The Medal for Distinguished Contribution to American Letters*. He has sold over 350 million books worldwide, but when he started writing he just wanted enough cash to pay for his rent. Fortunately, King loves writing. His habit of writing every day, even on holidays, eventually paid off to earn him a spot as one of the literary greats.

Why is it that we don't mind failing at work we don't like, but when it comes to work we love, we fear failing the most? If we refuse to fail at what we love, what else is there? And if we don't master what we love, what else is there?

When you learn to master the craft that is your true passion, you tap into the most diverse strength in your personal arsenal. When we commit to the process of winning first and stay that course, we can overcome any barrier that gets in the way.

I am always amazed that most people are willing to get up early, go to work for ten hours [including commute time], and then come home too exhausted to do the work that really matters. Yes, the reality is we have family, work and responsibility that has to be taken care of.

But what do you do when you are with real time on your hands? How do you spend those minutes or hours when you are free? Do you work on your passion, making time for it because it matters, or, would you rather watch television?

In many cases, it isn't that we lack time or motivation: it is commitment. Like Jordan, we have to get up early and commit to making the shots, hit or miss. It is the action of doing it that makes the difference.

If you have a passion you're hiding from the world, what are you waiting for? Permission to start building your dream? Nobody is going to give you permission to start living your dream. You are the one who has to jump in and take it. If you are waiting for the perfect time, you'll regret it years later, saying, "If only I had…"

Michael Jordan wasn't afraid of failing; he was only afraid of not doing what he loved. This is the case with many people. We are in a position where we work for other people and try to do a good job so we qualify for that paycheck. Then, when we get that paycheck, we feel validated, rewarded, fulfilled.

But it never lasts.

One of the surest roads to happiness is by doing what you love, and the only way to get there is by taking action, overcoming adversity, and charging ahead without looking back.

People are desperate to do what they love, but the problem is this: they are either too busy, or they don't yet know what it is they want to do so they do whatever job comes along. You might pay your bills by doing work that doesn't matter, but you'll always be poor if you end up with regret.

My big scare came one day when I realized nobody but me was in charge of my life. You see, for many years, I leaned on others for support. If I was in a relationship, I looked to that person for happiness. They never lasted because the relationship couldn't sustain my needs. What did I do then? I looked for another relationship. It was an endless series of failures. So, what is the definition of failing? Doing the same thing over and over again and expecting to get a different result. It never was different.

In past jobs I worked for a paycheck like everyone else. But, at the end of the month, having rewarded myself for a job well done by drinking away most of my earnings, I had more days left than cash. This is how we learn to fail, and keep on failing.

You know that Edison guy who loved to play with electricity? The story is, he failed 10,000 times. But by the end he had a successful product. Edison obviously had a massive amount of motivation to be persistent. If you can fail that many times and not give up, you are onto something. But we don't need to fail thousands of times. Just a few, or ten or twenty may be enough.

Show me a success story not riddled with failure. It doesn't exist. But I know many failures who never tried, and ended up burned-out, living futile existences for somebody else. If you enjoy working for someone else, building their brand, selling their products, and making money for them, then stop reading this book. Go back to doing that.

Or, if you are ready to stand up and take action towards doing the things you love, let's get to it.

Now...

Think about the amount of work the average person [you and I] put into working for other people or organizations. If you are doing work you don't like, you'll never get better at it unless you're forced to do so. Maybe your boss threatens to replace you if you don't meet sales goals. Or, maybe you won't get that promotion unless you can sign the contract with a big client.

I don't know much, but I do know this: work you love needs no prompting. You don't have to be threatened or be given ultimatums to succeed at what drives you.

Was Jordan forced to play basketball? No, he chose to play, and he decided to put in more effort than others.

When Stephen King was asked, "Why did you become a writer?" he responded with, "You think I had a choice?"

When we are made to do something, we don't put half as much effort in as we do when we're born to do it.

So now...

- Figure out what you love to do more than anything else. Invest your time on mastering this.
- Work out solutions to the obstacles that are holding you back.

The Four Rules for Succeeding at What You Love

(1). Commit to mastering your craft.

Spend time everyday working on the skill, technique, and know-how of your real work. Mastery doesn't mean perfection. It is what can be achieved with a lifetime of practice. We have to practice or there isn't any progress.

We master our passions by choosing to do whatever it takes to become better. If you have no time for practice, when can you find the time? I've heard people tell me all the plans they have for their lives after they retire. After they retire? What if you don't make it that far?

Many people die before they reach sixty. And if you do retire at that age, how motivated will you be to suddenly start working on your real dream? The time is now. The best time was yesterday, but if you're still thinking about finding the perfect time to get started, let me put this to rest right now.

Start today. Forget about *someday*. Life is full of someday promises. Someday I'll start that business; someday I'll take that trip; someday I'll change, and yes, someday we're all going to die. You might die with all those *someday* promises banked up.

(2). Benchmark your success against someone else.

Then, go above and beyond what they are doing. Pick someone you know that is succeeding at what you want to do. Make a list of their achievements and read about their successes and strategies so you can emulate what they've done.

Entrepreneur and the nation's #1 leading business strategist Tony Robbins said that we could achieve mastery by emulating those that have achieved what we want. This doesn't mean you'll get the same results—you probably won't—but doing what others do isn't a bad thing. Following in the footsteps of a successful person is much better than leading and being followed by twenty fools. You can benchmark your success by setting milestones for your work.

(3). Stay consistent with your practice.

Before we are good at something we have to be really bad at it. But many people start things they fail to stick with. I did this throughout my life and it became a bad habit I struggled to change.

Creating a consistent habit that focuses on learning one new skill is the key to mastery. Consistent practice with small improvements beats the 'I have to do this perfectly or else' way of thinking.

If you want to be a blogger, you have to post regularly and be satisfied with getting it done, even when it's not perfect. If you practice the guitar, you can focus on learning just one new chord a week. Practice just that one chord for thirty minutes a day. If cooking is your passion, make the same recipe every day for thirty days, tweaking it slightly differently each day so that you make gradual improvements to the taste.

Consistency, doing something regularly in small increments, is better than doing it once for four hours every other week.

We only master the things we pay attention to.

(4). Identify the areas that need the most attention and improvement.

One of the mistakes we make is recognizing what we can do well and doing more of it, while overlooking our weaknesses and convincing ourselves to let it go.

The master of any craft needs to be aware of what they do well and what needs improvement so they can excel at what they want to do. It isn't always fun or glamorous, but we have to work on our weaknesses as well as our strengths. This is how you carve out a life that is great instead of just good enough.

You don't want to settle for good enough. When we take the low road, and convince ourselves we have learned enough, we stop learning altogether. When we continue to learn, because we know that the world is unlimited, we keep making progress. When we move forward, we find fulfillment, satisfaction, and more happiness. Who doesn't want to be happy?

Key Takeaways

- Focus in on your true passion. Schedule thirty minutes a day to practice your craft.
- Fail at your passion and fail consistently. Our mistakes are stepping stones to progress.
- Don't settle for good enough. Identify the weaker areas of your life and focus on making it better.
- Develop the attitude of *I'm doing it now* instead of *I'm living scared.*

Practicing Limitless Thinking

"Keep on going and the chances are you will stumble on something, perhaps when you are least expecting it. I have never heard of anyone stumbling on something sitting down."

— Charles Kettering

Your thoughts are your most powerful tools. Everything you have and don't have can be linked back to your quality of thinking. Your limitations are directly linked to your thoughts. Just as you can limit yourself, the opposite can also be true. You can develop an abundance mindset, and when you believe anything is possible, your thoughts and the lifestyle they create become limitless.

But remember: just as positive thoughts can raise you up and make you feel like you're on top of the world, negative thoughts can drag you down to the bottom of the barrel. Negativity is the main source of fear. Positivity is the removal of fear.

Go Limitless

When you are in a negative state of mind, everything becomes twice as hard because you feed into your limitations and give them power. This is why we need to move away from negative thoughts and the people, places, and things that create them.

But don't just take my word for it; let's try an exercise. Clear your mind of whatever you are thinking right now. Sit in silence for five minutes. Now, think of something that excites you. Whatever it is, get passionate about it. Let it fire you up. Hold nothing back. Visualize yourself doing things that you once thought were impossible. When you can visualize yourself doing it, you will do it. Your vision for living a limitless lifestyle spills over into the real world.

For example, I am thinking about taking a family vacation. I can do this because I have my own business – all I need is my laptop and imagination. No cubicle, and no boss. When I think about this, I feel excited because I know it is possible. Several years ago, this was one of those impossible dreams. I was tied to a job with little vacation time. I couldn't afford to go. There wasn't time for that.

The limits that are forged in my mind become reality. Every time. This is an important lesson. If anything prevents you from taking action now, it is the limiting beliefs that say, *this isn't for you*, why don't you go do something more realistic.

But realism is dangerous. When we judge our dreams against the bar of what is reality, we push ourselves into a funnel of limitations. For example, to say that I will earn three thousand dollars next month is possible. It isn't a challenge because anybody can do this. But to say

I'll be earning twenty grand a month one year from now is, from the start, an unbelievable goal when it is grounded in reality. Why? Reality exists because someone else set the bar and they expect us to live by it.

When nothing scares you, go ahead and raise the bar accordingly. You decide what it is that's possible. You set your limitless boundaries. You challenge the reality that has been decided by the world and all its systems.

To be limitless, we must challenge the 'normal' way of thinking and set our beliefs outside the comfort zone. Most people won't do this. They're afraid to fail. But wouldn't you rather fail at something that is challenging and builds a new future than fail at what you hate doing? You can be limitless in your decisions and beliefs.

What is your biggest goal in life?

Is there someone you love and want to spend more time with?

Would you like to take a trip?

Is there a job you've hesitated to apply for but want more than anything? Can you visualize yourself in this position doing the work you love?

Now, write down an idea, dream, or concept that you've always believed is *beyond your current reality*. This should be a goal or life dream that appears to be beyond your reach. For example, maybe you want to create a company that earns you one million dollars a year, write a bestselling book, or travel the world as a digital nomad.

If you want to test your limitless thinking, tell people about your next big goal. You can quickly weed out the naysayers who will tell you it isn't possible. People will tell you it can't be done until somebody does it. When someone says this, just remember, what they mean is that it's not possible for them. But, for you, it is doable.

Becoming a limitless thinker doesn't require any special talent or ability. Remember: we are trained to think within our own limitations. When I was in school, many years ago, teachers told me what I could and couldn't do. Over time, if you believe in your limitations, every decision you make will be followed by a weak action. You'll never push yourself any further than you believe you are capable of.

Distance Yourself from Naysayers

People who are unsupportive of your limitless lifestyle and holding you back have no place in your life. You have two choices. You can: 1. Join them or 2. Distance yourself from them.

Hanging out with negative people makes you negative. When you are exposed to streams of negativity on a regular basis, even if it isn't by choice, you absorb the bad energy it sends your way. Naysayers stick together. If you are in a situation where you have to associate with them, distance yourself from them as much as possible.

People who grew up in negative, limiting environments struggle most of their lives to create a limitless mindset. It becomes a major hurdle to overcome an environment that focuses on promoting mediocrity and living within set boundaries and limitations. But this doesn't mean your life is an impossible gambit. You have the power to change your thoughts and emotions. You can't always change your environment, but you can control your reaction to it.

The same can be said for your work atmosphere. Each office has an overall culture that is created by the company executives, employees, and corporate mission. Depending on your work environment this may harm or help you. Again, we can't always choose the people we work with, but we can choose our attitude towards the situation. Your attitude is the one thing you have complete control over, regardless of other people who may drag you down.

Practice Limitless Mainstreaming Every Morning

Your thoughts are most influential first thing in the morning. In fact, if you wake up with thinking negative thoughts they might stick with you for the rest of the day. Start the day off right, and you'll have a much better chance of maintaining a positive mood throughout the day.

Spend the first 20 minutes of your day developing your thoughts and plans for the day. Here is what I do: block off twenty minutes after you first wake up. This is, possibly, the most important twenty minutes of your day. The quality of your day hinges on *how you wake up*.

Instead of rolling out of bed late and grabbing your smartphone, we are implementing a new strategy. This will change everything and build the foundation for limitless thinking.

In Hal Elrod's bestselling book, *The Miracle Morning,* he introduces the Life S.A.V.E.R.S. practices. I use the S.A.V.E.R.S. methods of **S**ilence, **A**ffirmations, **V**isualization, **E**xercise, and **R**eading to improve my thoughts for the day. Check out *The Miracle Morning* and put these strategies into practice.

I set up my limitless thinking for each day by **setting my thoughts straight before bed.** The last thought you had before crawling under the sheets is the first thought you'll have when you wake up. So, if you want to wake up early and make the most of your time, work on your thoughts for ten minutes before bed.

Four Simple Strategies

Go into Silence. Play a deep and relaxing piece of music. My favorite is *Weightless* by Marconi Union. Then, let your thoughts drift. This is a form of meditation but, instead of trying to think of nothing, you think of the good things in your life. This is how you can go into silence while making everything around you perfectly calm. The day's arguments, problems, and challenges can be washed away.

Start with Gratitude. Who do you feel deep gratitude for being in your life? What do you feel grateful for? Run through the most important people in your life. Think about them and send them positive thoughts.

I suggest you start each day with a gratitude list. It can be one thing or ten. Focus on the good people and things that are worth working for. Without gratitude, it's hard to practice a limitless way of life.

Self-Talk with Positive Affirmation. Over the years I have practiced recounting quotes and affirmations to change my thinking. This has a powerful impact on the way your mind functions. As I mentioned already, we all come with our own *self-talk radios* pre-installed in our minds.

Over the years, this radio gets louder and the noise increases with experience. If we don't closely monitor it, our radios can [and will] turn our thoughts into negative messages that impact our mental health.

An affirmation is a phrase that can change your beliefs. They work because we get so stuck in our own thoughts that we forget to correct course. The messages that we listen to become repetitive over time until we believe them. You have the power to choose your thoughts. Positive affirmations can help.

Read a Good Book. Kick-start your day by reading and thinking positively in the morning. If you start your day right, you'll do most things right. Start it badly, by focusing on resentment, and you'll feel like shit. Worse yet, you'll build fear and resentment into everything you do. Fear causes us to act out irrationally without thinking of the consequences.

Limited vs. Limitless

To expand your freedom and choices, you need to expand the limitless possibilities you believe in. It isn't so much what you believe, but how strongly you believe in it. Likewise, it isn't what you think, but how positively you think it. Abundance thinking, or limitless thinking, focuses on growth. Limited thoughts keep you scrambling for more because you feel restricted and limited to what is possible.

Our self-created limitations set the bar for success in all segments of our lives: financial matters, relationships, work, and personal development. By staying limited you are deciding how big, how far, and how much you can transform your life.

A limited thinking person struggles to come up with an occupation that pays six figures; whereas limitless people find new ways to increase income streams and work to reach their goal of a six-figure salary.

Building Abundance

Limited people live in a world of scarcity. They believe life is about holding onto their possessions. When they learn something, they'll keep it to themselves so nobody can take their idea and profit from it.

If you live in scarcity, there is never enough money, time, or material things to keep you satisfied for long.

Scarcity is about hoarding and skimping. Limitlessness is about giving and sharing. If there is any single mindset that creates a constantly fearful state, it is the mindset of scarcity.

Limitless people are focused on abundance. They believe the world is full of treasures, and that there is more than enough for everyone. There is enough money, food, shelter, and love to go around.

Abundant people live happier, healthier lives. They have little fear. When they do, the right people usually surround them. If you focus on the abundance and richness of what you have, and you grasp the large opportunity that is available, you'll see it is easy to create an abundant way of thinking. Abundance is, after all, a way of life, and has little to do with owning anything.

Key Takeaways

- When we are limitless in our thoughts, we also become limitless in our actions.
- Your actions will always follow your thoughts, so make your thoughts a positive driving force to get you to do things that matter most to you.
- Abundance isn't about having stuff, but, rather, giving stuff away. It isn't about owning, but about letting go. And it's not always about being the best, but about striving to make the best of a situation.
- Let go of scarcity thinking. It has no place in your life. Embrace the limitless lifestyle that is yours to create.

Rejecting the Life You Don't Want

"The greatest day in your life and mine is when we take total responsibility for our attitudes. That's the day we truly grow up."

— John C. Maxwell

In our day-to-day lives, it feels like everything is just happening around us without our input or effort. But actually, we create most of what is happening, even if it is at a subconscious level. Believe it or not, you have the power to structure everything to happen for you instead of to you.

In other words, we can be intentional about building the life we want. This is far better than accepting the life we've just fallen into by default.

For years, I lived passively and by default — I would just *go with the flow* or *take whatever comes*. The problem with this approach is that you give up control of the main events that shape, mold and transform your life. When I realized I was my life's creator and not just a passive participant reacting to circumstances, everything changed.

I learned to reject the life I no longer wanted. This included getting up every day, getting dressed, and commuting one hour to an office so I could sit at a desk and play with a computer. This meant no longer doing *their* work that I hated. Believe me, when you make the conscious choice to do something about your life's direction, it changes it all.

When you reject the life you have for the life you truly want, your mindset shifts from a passive state to pro active. In other words, you seize control of your life. This is something many people fail to do. We struggle, give up, fight some more, try to push through, and when we feel the pressure to conform, many of us feel defeated.

If this has happened to you, it's not your fault. Life can be tough. We try to keep our heads above water, but sometimes we're pushed below the surface. Instead of thriving we end up drowning in worry, stress, and the possibility of failure.

The Life You Build When You're Scared

We live in one of two realities: living scared or doing it scared. If you are still living scared, chances are somebody or something else has locked you into a life that has been crafted for their purpose. Again, it's not all your fault, so before you blame yourself for creating a bad situation, let's focus on turning it around.

I've been there many times. There are days when I am still caught in the tumultuous river of life and I think everything is pushing me under and that I'll never succeed. When I am trapped by my fear, I build a life and make choices that keep me stuck.

But, if I tap into the abundance that I am creating, I build the opposite lifestyle. When you take responsibility for where you are at, it becomes a journey with greater clarity. Instead of guessing what you should be working for, you know what it is you need to do.

Living scared creates hesitation. You feel uncertain about what you should be doing. You're afraid to take that next step for fear of screwing up, looking bad, or acting stupid. Feeling trapped, we stick to the safer path, but there is danger in safety for the fearful.

To live with less fear and gain greater courage for doing it scared, we must begin with intention.

This brings us to...

Building an Intentional Lifestyle

Many years ago, I found myself living a life that was no longer aligned with my dreams or future goals. My dream was still taking shape, but what I did know was that the life I had wasn't the life I wanted. So what did I do? I rejected the life I had made and set out to create a new one.

Oprah Winfrey did this. Born into poverty in Mississippi, she knew she didn't want to be trapped living the life she'd been born into, wearing potato sacks in place of clothes. Instead of accepting it, Oprah did something about it. She set out to carve her own destiny by becoming the world's most successful and wealthiest TV talent. None of this was by accident. Her life was built by intention. She knew precisely what she wanted and, more importantly, she knew what she didn't want.

Knowing what we don't want is as powerful as knowing what we do want. For example, maybe you want to write for a living and be a bestselling author, but you are currently working a job you don't like. The work isn't what you want to do. You know you want out, and by deciding, with intention, that you are going to break free and do the work you love, you create momentum to make changes and move toward doing the work you love.

Your intentional actions lead to desired results. When people do what is expected of them, because somebody else demands it, they lose that intentional mindset. But, staying focused on what you really want, even when others are trying to direct you, is how you break out of the life you don't want.

When you find yourself stuck in a situation that you had no intention of creating, then it's time to...

Saying NO to What You Don't Want

This is the key to rejecting the unwanted stuff that is thrown at you. Like prisoners forced to eat whatever is given to them, we think we have no choice in what life is offering. Do not settle for what you can get but rather, set out to attract and obtain those things that you really desire.

If you are not saying *yes* to what you want, you are saying *no* to what you do want. By saying *no* more often, you can stop saying *yes*. For years, I would say *yes* just to get along with people: my employer, my spouse, and even people I didn't know.

I would try to please people to earn their approval and look for their acceptance to feel complete. But this robs us of our personal freedom. Creating a lifestyle that is intentional has to start with intentional choices. It is easy to believe that we have no choices when, in reality, we have lots of choices.

But we limit ourselves to believing that *I have to do this* or *if I don't do this, someone will get upset*. You need to be crystal clear about what your actions lead to. This is intention. You have a desired outcome that you'll never reach if you play it safe all the time. When we play it safe to please somebody else, we risk more of our happiness in the long run.

A friend and mentor once said to me, "When you rock the boat, someone always gets wet. So, what are you waiting for? Tip that thing over!" What he meant was, if you want to get real results, you will have to break some eggs, but that's okay. It's better than walking on eggshells.

Take responsibility for your life: Yes, *your* life. Begin by recognizing the power of your decisions. You can choose, decide, and initiate action. If someone or something is getting in your way and keeping you from creating an intentional lifestyle, this is an obstacle that must be removed. When we fail to try to move the barriers in our life, we stay stuck in our ruts.

But, when you do things differently, not everyone likes the changes you make. Some people liked the old you; they needed you to hang out at the bar with them and complain about the misery of life. But when you shift your actions, it creates change. Courage is born from change, and change can come from courage.

Don't just settle for what you can get. Decide what you want, decide what you are willing to give up to get it, and then create a **massive action** game plan for getting it.

What to Do When You Are in Doubt

If you doubt what you are doing, ask someone you trust who has the success you are striving for. Don't ask the person who is failing their way through life. Ask the person you want to emulate — a mentor or coach — who is doing what you want to be doing. Ask someone who is leading with intention. Get real answers from the people who are leading by example. You can only succeed if you model success.

Streamlined actions in alignment with your intentional outcome won't fail you. But, follow the path of confusion and doubt and you'll encounter fear everywhere you turn. Fear is the result of not knowing if what you are doing is right or wrong. When you are not in control, meaning that something else is deciding your fate, you can expect to be fearful of today, tomorrow, and all the days to follow.

You have the power to reject the life that has been handed to you. We are not victims of our circumstances, but the masters of it. You control your future by managing your thoughts and actions. Manage them well because if you don't, somebody else will.

Key Takeaways

- Rejecting the life you don't want is about saying *no* more than you say *yes*. You have to say *no* to the people, situations, and distractions that steal your time and freedom.
- Confusion and chaos become your masters when you can't control your environment.
- Be intentional in your choices, actions, and behaviors.
- Choosing intentional direction puts you in charge of your life. What you do with intention directs your purpose.
- Focus on the obstacles blocking your path and discuss with your mentor the solutions for handling difficult situations.

"What Would My Life Be Like If...?"

In a workshop I attended several years ago, the facilitator asked us a question: "What would you do with your life from this day forward if you were no longer afraid?"

The next question was more shocking: "Where would you be in your life today if you had taken action years ago instead of living scared?"

We all knew the answer. We'd be someplace else doing what we love instead of in a workshop trying to figure it out. But it didn't matter. We were all on a journey together and, we all had to start where we were at that moment. At that time, I was with a group of other people trying to figure out where we would like to be in the not-too-distant future.

To break it down even more, we had to come up with specific scenarios that were holding us back. Some people feared starting a business, racing a triathlon, speaking in public, or meeting new people. The people who joined the seminar were all suffering from some form of *hold back.* They wanted to change or do something significantly different with their lives, and yet, something held them back from taking action.

Here is an example. One of the attendees, Bob, wanted to travel around the world, but he had never traveled before. He was afraid of planes and didn't even have a passport. He said that he always found lots of excuses to stay scared and do nothing. Over the course of the next day in the workshop, as each of us analyzed the fears that were keeping us scared to act, here is what we found out:

All of us agreed that we were focused on the big picture scenario. For example, several people wanted to start their own businesses but when they thought about all the work ahead—hiring employees, technical issues—they felt overwhelmed and would procrastinate. This was a common thread. We would visualize the outcome but lose sight of the small steps that lead up to it.

So how do you climb the world's tallest mountain?

You start from the base.

One step at a time.

One foot in front of the other.

You get there by keeping it simple.

Creating an If-Then Plan

To accomplish anything, you have to break down the action steps into bite-sized manageable chunks. This is the first stage to realizing your big goals.

In Bob's case, he wanted to travel, but he would have panic attacks when he thought about visiting other countries. So, he broke the process into manageable chunks. These were small steps he could focus on.

Instead of worrying about what he would say when he got to security at the airport, he would focus on the next step, such as applying for a passport or checking out the travel packages that he could purchase for his trip.

So, here's a list of his initial steps:

Step #1: Go to the passport office. Get a passport.

Step#2: Take a short trip on an airplane to a neighboring state.

Step #3: Research the first country to visit – only the first one.

Step#4: Make a list of activities and sites to see in that first country.

During this process, we were instructed to ask ourselves: "What if I just…" So in Bob's case, "What if I just get my passport first? What then?"

Getting a passport isn't a big deal; it's a relatively simple process. You don't have to think about the 30 countries you want to visit. That comes later. Just focus on the one thing that is getting you closer to that goal.

In many cases, people ask the wrong questions. They ask themselves scary questions that keep them from doing anything. For example, I used to ask myself: "What will happen if I fail? What will happen if I take the test and don't make it? What will happen if I lose money?" Every negative question receives a fearful answer.

But you can turn this around to your advantage as well.

What would happen if I lost money? Well, I would learn a valuable lesson. And besides, money can be replaced.

What would happen if I failed? Well, I'd learn what not to do next time. Or, maybe I'd discover a new way to fail. Every failure, as we've learned, is success in disguise. We learn by failing, and we can succeed faster by knowing what doesn't work.

If you imagine your actions failing, you'll never do anything. This is why people stay stuck. They are too frightened to move forward. Would you take action if you were convinced you'd lose money or something worse? Maybe not. But turn that vision into something positive and you can find a way.

What would happen if I...

- Made that phone call?
- Filled out that application form?
- Met that new person who is interested in a date?

- Tested out that new idea?
- Tried to implement that new habit?
- Signed up for the course?
- Visited the bank to enquire about house loans?

Don't hold back because you are scared. Everyone is scared. We're all afraid to fail, afraid to look stupid, or afraid to imagine the possibilities. But, people take incredible chances every day. They go beyond their comfort zones and do things that seriously impact their lives.

So, the question is: *what are you going to do today?*

What is on your *what would happen if I...* list?

Nobody has all the answers for what they should be doing with their life. But, you can think deeply about what your next step should be by asking yourself the question: *what would life be like if...* Then you can start to visualize the life you want to create.

We can't undo the past, but we can create a better tomorrow. We can create a future and all the things that come with it just by deciding. Once you decide, *commit* to your objectives. Know what your dream is. Then, *execute* your plan with massive action.

Finding Your Dominoes Trigger Point

Several years ago I was introduced to what is called the *domino effect*: one action can trigger everything else to fall into place.

Or, in the case of dominoes, one action [the first domino to fall] impacts all the other steps that follow [the rest of the dominoes fall]. When you take one action, it leads into another.

Soon you are full of **confidence** and you feel **unstoppable**. But it starts with taking action towards that first task.

Now, identify the *one thing* you can do to set off the series of actionable steps.

Here are some examples:

You want to write a book but you've been putting it off. So, you create a simple mind map. This leads to an outline. The outline leads to the first paragraph, page, and eventually the completion of the first chapter.

You want to run in a marathon, but you're a terrible runner. So, you set a goal to run five minutes, or 200 meters on the first day. The next day, you run 500 meters. You keep building on your previous day's goal until you are up to 5 km.

You want to start your own blog, but all the steps involved overwhelm you. So, first you register for a domain name. Then, you sign up for hosting. Then you watch a video on how to write your first blog post.

You want to travel, to expand your mind, and explore places you've only dreamed of, but you're afraid to get on that airplane. Can you imagine what would happen if you did?

I love the idea of reinventing and transforming one's life into what it could be instead of settling for what it is. When we stay scared and love scared, we settle for what is. There is no growth. No stimulation. We need to take action and make a difference.

Change is always frightening. But what is scarier is not changing, staying stagnant, and failing to pursue your life goals because you're afraid of what might happen.

If you were being chased by a lion right up to the edge of a cliff, and your only chance of survival was to jump, you probably would. In times of stress we take action to survive. But daily life isn't much different. We should jump into unknown waters so we can find out what is on the other side of our fear.

Again, all of this is possible if you keep asking yourself: *what if I just...* And then you go and do it. This could be considered your most difficult task for the day as well. If you are going to start your day right, why not start by taking action towards your dream.

You have nothing to lose and nothing to fear.

What would you do if you finished this book and discovered the secret to setting your dreams on fire?

Let's find out.

Key Takeaways

- Make a list of actions you have been meaning to take and ask yourself: *how would life be different if I did this thing?*
- What are you scared of trying? What negative outcome are you holding onto? Turn this outcome into something positive and see how it affects your emotions.
- What is the one massive step you could take that would trigger your dominoes effect?
- Make a list of things that you can do by asking yourself: *What if I just...*
- Think baby steps. Take small, incremental actions towards your goal. Focus on moving forward just a little bit one small step at a time.

Tackling Your Most Difficult Tasks First

"Permanence, perseverance and persistence in spite of all obstacles, discouragements, and impossibilities: It is this, that in all things distinguishes the strong soul from the weak."

— Thomas Carlyle

An important part of the *Nothing Scares Me* formula is tackling the tasks, projects, or actions you have identified as most difficult and doing them first. When we take care of the tough stuff before anything else, we can exponentially reduce our level of fear. This eliminates procrastination and builds real momentum for the road ahead.

Working Through the Tough Stuff First

It is always easier to do the little things first — to do what is easy and then make time for the more difficult projects later. There is logic in this plan, but it fails for several reasons. First of all, we are creatures of comfort. The only time we do the tough stuff first is when we are forced to.

- Your boss gives you a deadline and makes you do that report by Friday.

- The bank tells you to pay your bill by this date or else they will cut off your credit.
- You have until this Friday to make that all-important call or you lose the deal of a lifetime.

In examining the things that you've swept under the rug, you may find a lot of projects, tasks, and forgotten deadlines. These tasks were left behind because, for one reason or another, we didn't want to do them.

I know what it is like when you have to do a job or task you don't want to. Let's be honest, when we don't want to face the reality of a situation, we will find a way to get around it. Most people take the *Ostrich Method* that I mentioned at the beginning of this book, when they are faced with difficult tasks. It is always *easier* to turn away when faced with a difficult challenge. We want to pretend it isn't there, as if by avoiding it, somehow it will just *take care of itself*.

People who deny their fear become a slave to it. Even if you ignore reality, it will still hit you full force one day, knocking you down for good. This is why getting into the habit of doing tough tasks first will make you mentally sharper, reduce anxiety, and increase your confidence in ways that you've never experienced. But it starts with you pulling your head out of the sand.

For years, I lived like an ostrich. I avoided tasks I didn't want to do. This included everything from controlling my finances to applying for a new passport. There were times I had to organize my life so I could function more efficiently, but I continued to put it off. The result: confusion, stress, fear, and personal anarchy.

You will never find peace by trying to escape your reality. There will always be something pulling at you when you leave business unfinished. Unfinished business can be anything from clearing your house of clutter to setting up your online business. If something sticks in your mind and refuses to leave, it's an indication that it needs to be done. If you're a procrastinator who fears taking action, this chapter is for you. Keep reading.

How Can I Finally Take on Difficult Tasks I've Been Avoiding?

Each night you could make a list of the top five tasks you want to get done the next day. Then, choose the toughest thing on your list. This is easy to determine because it's the one you don't want to do but must get done. You will try to resist this one thing the most. You'll find excuses not to do it and try to do the easy tasks first. Then the tough task will get moved down the ladder until, eventually, it's put aside until it rears its ugly head again.

Taking care of tough business reduces the fear factor exponentially. I suffer from severe stress and worry when I put things off that need to be done. You can lose sleep, lose hair, and lose money, too. But it doesn't have to be this way. The after effect of doing what scares you is powerful. The act of completing something gives you new perspective. You prove to yourself that the fear of starting was what you were hiding from.

My Simple System for Getting Difficult Tasks Done

First of all, it comes down to how you identify your action steps. If this were something that could be done in thirty minutes, I would do it right away. But some of our tough tasks require in-depth planning, systematic organization, and weekly goals. This is why we put things off: we have too many things to think about in a world full of distraction.

Worse yet, the things I was neglecting were important, but I continued to chase the *easy rabbits*, thinking I was making progress. What feels like efficiency is, at times, really the illusion of covering up what should be done in favor of what we want to do. When you develop the habit of *Doing It Scared*, you put yourself on a course to achieve your goals faster, and focus your energy on more important projects while eliminating the unnecessary. You can stop wasting valuable time on the activities that matter least.

Start with Your Project List

As David Allen writes in his book, *Getting Things Done,* a project is anything that requires more than three steps. If we have a set of tasks we need to perform, set aside time every day, even if it is just ten minutes, to knock off the mini-goals to get the big project done.

But first, you need to *make a list of projects*. What is on your plate that will be completed with a series of steps?

Chances are there is a list of multiple action steps to go along with each project. Without knowing what needs to be done, we can easily get bogged down and overwhelmed. Then, the cycle of doing things by default is picked up again.

Here is a list of projects that are hovering over my head and filling my mental space with clutter.

Create a new website. I procrastinated for almost one year, potentially costing myself thousands of dollars by having no place to sell products or services.

Write a book. I have always wanted to write a book. Although I have five written now, this was a huge undertaking when I started mostly because I feared the rejection that could come from selling a real product.

Declutter my home. There is nothing worse than wading through junk every day. And it's easy to turn a blind eye and just toss stuff in the corner. Clutter creates stress, and stress leads to fear, worry, and anxiety. This is a major project, but the more you tackle it, the easier it becomes.

There are many tasks we put off because they are difficult, but the main reason we stress is scarcity.

I was always afraid of starting things I could not follow through, or of becoming overwhelmed by the amount of work and giving up.

To get cracking on the difficult tasks holding you back, create a list. It is this list that is going to show you what you have been neglecting. Now, this is not a to-do list. We don't want to make a list of things we should be doing [such as picking up the groceries or signing up for Netflix]. This is the list of what scares you. There should be nothing easy on it. The golden rule is that when you struggle or don't want to put something on this list you need to.

A to-do list is simple. We usually write down tasks we'd like to do, and they are usually unproductive. Your *tough tasks* list is different. It should make you uncomfortable. Mine did. But as I approached each obstacle, and set out to tackle the action steps for each project, I became empowered in a way I want you to feel.

So, Let's Get to It...

You can use software to record and track your steps, or plain old pen and paper. I may be old fashioned, but I like pen and paper. There is something about writing it down that makes it more real. Write your list and tack it up on your wall. Don't file it away where you can't see it or you'll forget about it within a week.

Start your list with a mind dump of all the difficult tasks you have been putting off, neglecting, or avoiding. This list needs to be a hard version of the truth.

Maybe you've been putting off having a serious conversation with someone because you don't want to rock the boat or cause trouble. Once again, if it's on your mind, it needs to be done. No exceptions. This work is, perhaps, the most important task-based activity in this book. I don't say that lightly. When we take action in the *moments we feel scared,* it builds greater courage to confront uncomfortable situations.

When I decided to do the stuff I'd avoided for years, it was as if I was setting myself free. The things that you bury, even though they may benefit you in the long run, are not going to disappear. Remember, life is going to pass even if you choose the ostrich approach and bury your head in the sand. You can hide but you can't escape.

So, make your list. Then divide it into two parts. After you complete your brain dump, take a look and see what tasks are actually projects. Then, create a folder for projects. If you are writing this down, use a whole sheet of paper for each project. Like I said, I get more out of it if I write everything in a notebook. You can type it up later if you want.

Now, a project is anything that requires multiple steps. If you want to set up a website for an online business, this requires several steps and weeks of work. Maybe you've been avoiding it because tech stuff scares you, or you are worried that after you get it all done nobody will come knocking on your virtual door. I know, the fear holds you back, but I encourage you to push forward. You'll only regret it if you don't try.

You can make another list for actions that can be completed in less than thirty minutes. If you have several projects, you'll have a lot of action tasks that will take thirty minutes or less. But, we want to do this separately. Individual items that can be completed [and that are not projects] can be on your other list.

Now You Have Two Lists — One for Short Tasks, One for Projects

The project lists will work like this. You are taking a 30,000-foot view of the scope of this project, and you'll spend some time mind dumping actions required to complete the project. Depending on the scope of the project this may take some time, but this is the best way to get this done. Then, you can easily show up every day, pull out your list of action tasks, and put your plan into action.

For years, I avoided doing certain projects because I was clueless about what actions needed to be taken. I was looking at the project as a huge behemoth that existed in my mind only. Without an organized plan, you'll struggle to tame your scared factor. There is nothing like getting things done and feeling that sense of deep accomplishment that comes with completion.

So, if you are ready, get to work creating your action plan. This doesn't have to be finished today, but this is what I recommend.

If you follow my advice, you'll nail this.

Set aside one day – one *whole* day. Dedicate it to mapping out your projects, writing action plans, and determining how many hours will be required to get it done.

Doing it in one day is better than stretching it out over several days or weeks. I discovered that, when I didn't do it in one day, it dragged on for months, and, eventually, I stopped altogether and nothing got accomplished.

Block off one day to make a master list of both:

1. Projects + action items for each project;

2. Tasks that can be finished in 30 minutes or less.

That is it.

By making this exercise a priority, you'll reduce your fear, feel less scared about waking up in the morning, and gain greater control over a part of your life that has been out of control.

Key Takeaways

- Create a master list of your difficult projects and tasks.
- Set aside an entire day for this work.
- Choose the project you are going to work on first.
- Make sure it is one that you've been putting off.

Building Confidence
(The "Brick-by-Brick" Builder Strategy)

> *"Action is a great restorer and builder of confidence. Inaction is not only the result, but the cause, of fear. Perhaps the action you take will be successful; perhaps different action or adjustments will have to follow. But any action is better than no action at all."*
>
> **— Norman Vincent Peale**

In this final chapter of *Nothing Scares Me,* I'll share with you the **four barriers** that defeat your confidence. Then, I'll follow up with the **six strategies** you can implement to increase your confidence to an all-new level.

But first, it is critical that I explain the key foundation of building and maintaining a life of confidence. There are four things we need to deeply consider when focusing on confidence building:

1. Confidence building is an internal job. Yes, your environment and the world around you have a heavy influence, but, at the end of the day, you are responsible.
2. Confidence building is a system of slow gains [more on this in a few pages].

3. Confidence is a learned condition. We can train ourselves to be as confident as we want. How confident would you have to be to tackle your biggest goal this year?
4. Confidence must be grounded in reality. If you tell yourself you are a super athlete and that you're in great shape in order to boost your confidence, but, in fact, you smoke and are overweight, you have to bring yourself down to reality and start with the truth of where you are.

> *"Confidence is, after all, your ability to believe in yourself. It is the highest form of self-esteem. Without believing in what it is you want to achieve, you'll fail to achieve it. When you believe, it kicks your internal power into hyper drive. A powerful belief can overcome any obstacle and pave the way for better things to come your way."*
>
> **— Patrick King**

I'm going to share with you some powerful but simple strategies for building confidence. But first, 5 obstacles that get in the way of confidence development.

The Four Obstacles That Kill Confidence

I've suffered from a lack of confidence most of my life. I used to think I was born with some kind of ailment that nobody else had, because I had very little confidence in anything. I would read stories about brave people and how they overcame insurmountable obstacles to achieve their dreams.

Later, after a lot of self-searching, I discovered that it wasn't the lack of anything that was the problem, and my external environment had very little to do with it. It's what I was holding onto that was killing my confidence.

The barriers I created in my own mind were holding me back. It was then I realized that change always happens on the inside first.

Although we are influenced by external events that we have little control over, we have total power over the internal conditions that govern our thoughts and feelings.

When we struggle to overcome a barrier in our lives, in most cases, the walls are built on the inside. This is where we keep our fears and doubts locked away. When you can recognize the obstacles in your way as something you created, it is easier to remove them.

Here are four obstacles that could be holding you back from being more confident.

1. Uncertainty & Self-doubt

Having little faith in our capabilities or skills, we fill ourselves up with feelings of doubt and uncertainty. We use language like, *I can't do this* or, *how will I ever get through this?* When you have an image of yourself as someone who *can't*, this means you usually won't. As I already discussed in chapter 7, self-doubt can be turned into confident action by doing what you are afraid of.

The courage is on the other side of your actions. When you are feeling uncertain and doubtful of what you should do next, it's an indication that fear is holding you back. In all likelihood, if you question your self-doubt, you may discover that it is being created by your lack of belief.

2. Perfectionistic Thinking [all-or-nothing]

This kills your confidence because it prevents you from ever starting anything. Perfectionism is closely tied with procrastination. When we fear not doing it perfectly, we begin to fantasize about what it would be like if we did do it. Or worse yet, you are waiting for the perfect moment before taking action.

But as we now know, the only path to building real confidence that sticks is to do it: 1. When you are scared, and 2. Frequently. Confidence isn't something you can build up by dreaming about it, and you'll never have that perfect condition or situation. The time is and always has been right NOW.

3. Focusing Only on the Big Win

Can you imagine if the only time you ever felt good about yourself was when you accomplished something BIG. For example, you might feel confident after making that huge sale, but what about all the little sales you had to make to build up to it? We often dismiss the little steps we take to get to where we want to be.

Before you can run a full marathon [42.195 km], you have to be able to run five km, then ten, and eventually build yourself up to running the entire distance. But those little distances are, in fact, goal achievements. Getting closer to the BIG goal builds your confidence along the way. The road to success, whatever that may be, is littered with small victories.

4. Believing In F.E.A.R.

When we believe that our fears are greater than we are, it makes them larger than life. Our fears are not bigger than we are but, believing that they can defeat us, adds weight to the illusion of fear. Throughout this book I discussed several anecdotes to overcoming our fears and doubts and, to keep fear in perspective, we need to look at this way.

Fear is nothing more than **F**alse **E**vidence **A**ppearing **R**eal. Many of the future events we are convinced will happen rarely do. Sure, bad stuff does happen, and in many cases the things we never feared could happen too.

For example:

- You lose a job you were convinced was secure. What are you going to do?
- Your spouse walks out on you after twenty years of marriage. What are you going to do?
- The market crashes overnight and you lose 90% of your investments. What are you going to do?

The truth is, we waste too much time dreaming up fears of the future that may or may not happen. But who can predict what is going to happen today, tomorrow or in

168 • SCOTT ALLAN

twenty years from now? There is no evidence to prove that 99% of our fears exist. The imagination is great at conjuring up illusions of what could happen.

The fear of failure? Yes, you will fail.

The fear of loss? Yes, you will lose something at least once in the next decade.

The fear of dying? Yes, that will happen too. Not today but, you can take great comfort in knowing most of your fears are false and some are destined to happen no matter what.

Our fears are only as great as our imaginations allow them to be. By knowing you can take action and make choices in the present moment, it fills your mind and spirit with confidence.

Building Confidence

This is, what I like to call, the **brick-by-brick method of confidence building**. For every mini-action you take, no matter how minuscule it may be, you are adding a small brick to your house of confidence. A home is really the combination of thousands of parts all glued, nailed, and pasted together. Those parts all got put together because somebody took the time to ensure every piece was installed.

What we can do, when it comes to building confidence, is, take a small action each day. This builds confidence while reducing the fear factor. And fear thrives in an environment when the person feels helpless, paralyzed, hopeless or out of control.

In **Barrie Davenport's** book _Building Confidence_ she says:

> "Your self-esteem is based on your beliefs about your own inherent values as a person and your emotional view of those beliefs. You can certainly lack confidence and still have self-esteem. It's much more difficult to lack self-esteem and still feel confident about yourself and your abilities."

Now, here are six strategies you can use to build your confidence, take action, and do the things you've always wanted to.

Strategy #1: Model the Confidence of Confident People.

Confidence is not just a one time and it's over event. It is an ongoing process and self-development. No matter how confident you are, there is always someone who is more so. They have more confidence because they are operating on a different level than you. They may be more experienced, wiser, more positive, or more influential in their fields. This is a good thing. It means that we can get there, not by achieving one massive win, but by achieving a series of small and incremental wins over a period of time.

By modeling the people who are achieving the incredible success we would like, we set the bar and push ourselves to reach for it. For example, I have fear of public speaking. When I get up on the stage in front of a crowd, fear grips my chest and I can barely breathe. BUT, I can build confidence in public speaking by watching others do it. How do they perform? What voice control are they using? How are they thinking in that moment as they are up on stage?

I can learn to be confident on stage by emulating the speeches of others – like by watching YouTube videos and then practicing in the mirror. You can apply this strategy to anything you desire to master and gain greater confidence.

You want to write a book but have no confidence in your writing? Read a book by your favorite author and then write a page on your thoughts about that book. Modeling isn't about copying but watching how others do it and then trying it ourselves with a twist of our own to make it unique.

Strategy #2: Start Small, Aim High.

Stephen Guise has written a book called *Mini-Habits*. In the book he discusses how we can get more done and achieve our goals, by doing things that matter and taking action in small bite-sized chunks.

By breaking down the process into smaller, manageable pieces, we reduce that overwhelming feeling of trying to achieve a major goal or break a bad habit. This also helps with building confidence of course because we can feel better about ourselves when we achieve each little goal.

Strategy #3: Practice to Fail First

In most cases we are so afraid to fail that we avoid trying. Our expectations and attitude from the get-go is: I have to be perfect before I try this. When we think this way, it reduces our motivation and drive to try. We defeat ourselves by refusing to practice and learning to fail.

If you play something, like the piano or guitar, you know that it takes years of failing and practice before you feel confident enough to play in front of a crowded room. Nobody gets it right the first time.

If you don't give yourself that room to grow, you'll never develop the skills you need to become confident. Learning to fail is essential. You need to give yourself permission to learn. Confident people are not born, they are made through years of trial and error.

Strategy #4: Perform the Small Stuff with Consistency

The next strategy is a combination of the first two but is a necessary element in the confidence formula. As I mentioned, confidence building is a consistent series of actions performed gradually over time. We build confidence by doing, regardless of the outcome. You will try many things and fail, but that also makes you stronger.

By performing small steps regularly, as in conditioning for a full marathon, your confidence is kicked up a notch with each mini-win. Don't stay focused on the big picture [finishing a full marathon], but on the bite-sized goals you have to hit to get there —such as running your first 2km.

The other key to this is that the action has to be consistent. If you are only practicing when you feel like it or are motivated to, confidence levels will fall. And if you fail to achieve your BIG WIN, such as completing that marathon, it will register as a failure in your mind. Stay consistent in your actions and set up a regular schedule for taking action.

Strategy #5: Focus on Confident Relationships

The people you hang out with, as we discussed in Chapter 3, have powerful influence on your confidence. If you are hanging with doubters and negativity mongers, you can expect to function at their level of self-esteem.

Make time for people who fill you up with that loving feeling and are good influencers. These people are your key relationships. You can gradually cut the people who keep you stuck loose.

These are the complainers, the people with heavy baggage, and the energy drainers. Cut them loose. Focus on the people who support and encourage your success. Recognize who they are and schedule quality time with them.

Strategy #6: Make a List of Your Good Stuff

Confidence is built when we focus on the positive aspects of our lives. You should start every week with a list of the five things you consider to be most important. Is it your family? Your health? Your business? What do you feel deep gratitude for? What makes you feel good?

You can start energizing your confidence right away by making a list of the people and things that you are grateful for. Gratitude is powerful. It puts the positive into perspective.

Go ahead and make your list right now. Then, let it be the first thing you read every morning. As time goes on, add to this list. Make it a goal to come up with a list of 100 items.

The Cost of Having Low Confidence

You have to ask yourself: *what is having a lack of confidence actually costing me?* Think about this for a minute. When we lack the confidence we need to reach out to people, we are missing out on valuable relationships that could help us on the journey. I'm a firm believer that nothing matters more than the relationships you develop along the way.

Developing confidence takes time, but it doesn't have to become a major project. It isn't something that you do just once and then forget about for the rest of your days.

Confidence building involves staying on track with your values, taking consistent small actions, and persevering to make gradual progress in relationships, work, and fun. Self-confidence is an inside job. You get there by working from the inside out.

This book is packed with enough to fill up your confidence meter and keep you charging forward and enjoying life.

Remember to laugh.

Enjoy what you have.

Reach out to others.

Give away what you have.

You can achieve anything by teaching other people how to reach their dreams, too.

Key Takeaways

- Most obstacles we encounter are created from the inside. You have complete control over the internal barriers holding you back.

- Most external situations are created by events beyond our control, and focusing on the barriers you can't destroy is a waste of time and effort.

- Self-doubt can be turned into confident action by doing what you are afraid of.

- The best time to act is NOW. In taking action we condition ourselves to push through even when we are faced with heavy resistance. If you're not moving forward, you are being held back.

- You can increase confidence by modeling confident people. How do they speak, act and perform?

- Build your confidence in learning to fail. Success is not the only way to become more confident. We get this way through attempting what we are afraid of, regardless the outcome.

- Stick with your values and take small, consistent actions every day until you get to where you want to be.

CONCLUSION

Weighing the Risks of Staying Scared

"Most people talk about fear of the unknown, but if there is anything to fear, it is the known."

— Deepak Chopra

We have come to the end of the book, but your journey is just beginning. Confronting your fears takes courage. Taking action, even when you are met with heavy resistance, is a matter of pushing forward with courage.

The people who persevere, stick to their plans, and take small steps to reach their goals, are the winners who never quit. As you will see, anyone or anything that tries to hold you back will fail. The quality of your lifestyle is everything. There is nothing you can't do when you stay committed to a course of action.

What are You Giving Up to Stay Scared?

As I promised, now that you have finished this book, you are ready to do anything. Nothing is standing in your way except *you*.

Anything worth having requires an element of discomfort. It means facing the things that scare us, and it requires working through your fears on a consistent basis. Never stop learning. Welcome the discomfort of being scared and doing something about it.

I want you to know that there is no shame in being scared. We all have fear. What matters is what we do with that fear. Will you stand back and let it control you? Or, will you get out there and take charge of your life by doing what needs to be done?

You know by now that you are capable of achieving anything. But don't take my word for it. Take action and get results. Don't be afraid to **live larger than life**.

What Action Should I Take?

First, make a list of all the things you've been putting off. Areas of procrastination point to something you fear — you either fear starting it, doing it, or completing it.

As part of your *Nothing Scares Me* action plan and to hold yourself accountable each day, I encourage you to do what you are afraid to do. Take a real look at your life, and, observing yourself carefully, take note of the tasks and situations you are avoiding. How would your life be different if you take action today, and do something that you have always been afraid to do?

By using this method, I have seen people leave jobs they hated, divorce abusive and controlling partners, and make total life changes by changing their bad habits, unhealthy behavior and self-defeating daily rituals. In order to change your life, you have to shift your approach to life.

Decision drives behavior. Behavior forges character. Character is mastered when we push through our greatest struggles.

Focus on Your Gains and Not the Goal

Every little success is a victory. But when we are working toward our dreams, it is easy to focus on the end goal. The problem is that it makes the journey seem too long. This journey is never-ending. I hope you'll never stop growing, pushing forward, and working towards your life-long ambition, whatever that may be.

As you grow, change, and develop, remember to focus on the small gains. Measure your success with the little stuff you accomplish every day. I find that when I focus on the big picture, I become overwhelmed with multiple action tasks that appear endless.

Keep track of the small stuff you get done. When you do something that challenges a fear or pushes you closer to your goal, that mini-victory is big. No matter what you are striving for, you can only get there by taking a series of small leaps and bounds.

I don't know a lot but I do know this: our lives are short, and some are much shorter than others. This is why we must appreciate every day. You were brought into this world for a reason. Aren't you the least bit curious to know what it is?

I know I am, and I try to uncover a bit of this treasure every day. I try to discover something new and do what part of me may want to resist creating more abundance in my life and the lives of others.

Don't stop jumping. You can sit on the ledge and look off in the distance toward what you have yet to climb, but, sooner or later, you have to start moving. Don't stop pushing forward. Break your resistance and seek help in the areas of your life that you struggle with.

Be afraid but courageous.

You've got this.

One step at a time...

Scott Allan

"When you walk to the edge of all the light you have and take that first step into the darkness of the unknown, you must believe that one of two things will happen. There will be something solid for you to stand upon or you will be taught to fly."

– Patrick Overton

CRUSH YOUR NEGATIVE BEHAVIOR

RELAUNCH YOUR LIFE

BREAK THE CYCLE OF SELF-DEFEAT, DESTROY NEGATIVE EMOTIONS, AND RECLAIM YOUR PERSONAL POWER

SCOTT ALLAN

Relaunch
Your Life

BREAK THE CYCLE OF SELF DEFEAT,
DESTROY NEGATIVE EMOTIONS, AND
RECLAIM YOUR PERSONAL POWER

Scott Allan

"The world breaks everyone, and afterward, some are strong at the broken places."

— **Ernest Hemingway**

The Struggle to Be Good Enough

"The secret of change is to focus all of your energy, not on fighting the old, but on building the new."

— Socrates

Do you ever have that feeling deep inside that you're just not good enough? Are you constantly comparing yourself to other people and coming up short? Are you trying to achieve success but end up feeling unfulfilled, unhappy, and undeserving of your accomplishments?

If you can relate to this, you're not the only one. I, and a great many others, know how you feel. I have experienced all of these things. Throughout my teachings, friendships, interviews, and coaching, I have met thousands of people just like you who have stopped to ask this one critical question:

"Am I good enough?"

Most of my life, I have lived with the core belief that I needed validation, acceptance from others, and a résumé of personal achievements in order to qualify as a person of real worth. The problem with this strategy is that I was looking outside of myself for validation.

If someone thought I had worth, I was worthy. If they didn't like me or treated me badly, it was because I deserved it. When I was rejected, it must have been because I had little to offer. As a result, I adopted a lifestyle of negative patterns and self-defeating behaviors.

Struggling with deep-seated emotions of defectiveness, low self-esteem, isolation and the fear of rejection, I had reached a point in which my very existence was dependent on the thoughts, opinions, and behavior of those around me. I was always trying to please people in order to gain approval. I wanted permission to be someone of importance.

Over time, I developed a sense of self-loathing as I became convinced that I had been born with serious flaws. I questioned many things about my existence. What I eventually discovered wasn't what I expected.

In trying to hide my flaws, I developed escape and avoidance tactics to cope with the fear and feelings of isolation, vulnerability, and deep-seated rejection issues that made relationships very difficult. This book is based largely on those experiences and the strategies I used to heal from negative emotions that were damaging my way of life.

In *Relaunch Your Life,* I am taking you on a journey of self-discovery. The goal is to target your self-destructive patterns and disprove their validity in order to live a more fulfilling, happier, and freedom-rich lifestyle.

Our negative patterns, thoughts, and behaviors keep us trapped, miserable, and frustrated. The steps in this book encourage you to take intentional action, recognize your negative patterns, and then apply strategies for personal recovery.

Relaunch Your Life will help you move you from a place of perfection toward imperfection, and convert negative emotions holding you back to positive emotions that are focused on self-love and the ability to accept who you are as a person. As we will discover together, it is not the world that has to treat us better. We must treat ourselves with respect, acceptance, and ultimately, self-love.

In developing yourself from within, and strategically targeting the negative behaviors and patterns keeping you trapped, you will discover how to:

- Overcome feelings of defectiveness
- Handle the fear of rejection and inferiority beliefs
- Break the cycle of self-defeat that is keeping you trapped
- Learn to trust yourself and others
- Reinvent your lifestyle and change the way you are living
- Confront your fears of vulnerability

- Become more confident with eye contact and body language
- Stop comparisons that are ruining your self-esteem
- Build a positive self-image of who you want to be
- Interact directly with people without feeling overwhelmed
- Stop feeling inferior to everybody you meet
- Put an end to comparing yourself to people who you think are better off than you
- Achieve greater satisfaction and fulfillment in your personal relationships

Who This Book Is For

Relaunch Your Life discusses how we tend to grapple with our true selves. This is more than just a book geared toward building confidence. The goal is to get to the heart of why people struggle through life, giving up on their cherished dreams in the midst of setbacks.

If you feel stuck in your life and you're looking for a way to move forward, this book is for you. If you are tired of being fearful around people, and you want to raise your confidence to a level you've only imagined, this book is for you. If you want to stop acting out the same negative beliefs, habits, and patterns day in and day out, then yes, this book is for you.

Case Studies

Throughout the book, I will refer to case studies to explain points and content. I am not using real names. Those mentioned are friends, coaching clients, or acquaintances I have met over the years and who shared their personal stories with me. Names have been changed to protect their identities.

Your Emotional Therapy Guide

This book was written with you in mind, the reader and student. I want to help you through your struggle so that you emerge stronger, better, and reinvented, confidently creating a path toward true healing. If you are feeling damaged inside, that's okay. You are stronger than you think you are.

The road to emotional recovery is a wonderful path, and I want you to join me on this journey. It is never too late to start over, and it's always the right time to *Relaunch Your Life*. It is how we come to terms with ourselves and our self-defeating habits. You will learn to live again, thrive by performing at your best, and do all the things you have always dreamed of doing. I wrote this book to teach you how to get there, and with this program, we can do it together.

The material in this book is designed to help you discover who you really are and how best to express your needs and desires without feelings of shame or guilt. Furthermore, I hope to show you a better way to live by chipping away at the self-defeating barriers in your path.

About Scott Allan

My name is Scott Allan, and I am an author, speaker, and coach. I help people overcome life's roadblocks and develop greater levels of confidence, reinventing their lives through actionable strategies that focus on never-ending self-improvement.

I am not a psychoanalyst or psychologist, but what I have to offer you are a lifetime of experiences and helping people to achieve their seemingly impossible dreams. I share these experiences with you in my books, coaching, and workshops.

No More Escape

Escapism is a skill that I picked up when I was a kid. I was never good at schoolwork, so I escaped from doing homework with TV and video games. I was shy and awkward throughout school so I escaped by rebelling and acting out.

The teachers labeled me a troublemaker. I was seeking attention to cover up for the parts of me that weren't functioning well. Feeling defective and unworthy, I fueled these negative beliefs through self-sabotaging tactics.

Nobody is perfect and we all move through life the best we can. Sometimes we fumble through it and other times we just fall down and struggle to get back up again. I've watched other people repeat the same mistakes over and over because they were trapped in a self-defeating pattern that was destroying their chances at success, yet they had no idea. They were too focused on blaming to see that they had the biggest role of all in contributing to their failure.

You can heal the wounds of the past and create a new life for yourself. In *Relaunch Your Life*, you're making a firm decision to do things differently, to take a different approach and shift your mindset from one of defeat to exercising personal power in your choices and actions.

How to Use This book

This book is set up to move you, both emotionally and mentally, from a place of pain to a higher plateau of personal power. To do that, I have set up the content and chapters so that each idea and the stories introduced build on each other from the beginning.

1. Take notes as you go or highlight the text on your e-reader or computer. Note-taking is a powerful method for reinforcing what you are learning.

2. Start from the beginning. It will just make more sense that way.

3. Talk with a close friend or family member about your progress. I find that including others in your journey of self-discovery is a positive way to stay connected with yourself.

4. Throughout this book, I will refer to emotional issues and addictions. If you struggle with these things, it is recommended that you seek professional help, a support group, or at the very least, a trusted friend.

Now, are you ready?

The days of living defeated are over.

194 • SCOTT ALLAN

It is time to be *good enough* for anybody or anything.

Let's *Relaunch Your Life* and make it everything you've ever dreamed it could be.

—Section 1—
Embracing the Fire

"Something very beautiful happens to people when their world has fallen apart: a humility, a nobility, a higher intelligence emerges at just the point when our knees hit the floor."

— Marianne Williamson

CHAPTER 1

The 6 Roadblocks That Keep Us Trapped

"When we are sure that we are on the right road there is no need to plan our journey too far ahead. No need to burden ourselves with doubts and fears as to the obstacles that may bar our progress. We cannot take more than one step at a time."

— **Orison Swett Marden**

In this chapter, we will take a look at the roadblocks that are keeping us trapped in a repetitive cycle of negative patterns. Before any real change can take place, we have to recognize the obstacles standing in our way. Then you can identify with what is holding you back and remove these barriers when they show up.

The Struggle with Change

If you've ever tried to shift a habit or behavior, like most people, you probably failed several times before succeeding. Change takes time, consistent effort, patience, and ongoing support from other people.

Standing between you and the life you want are a series of barriers set up to push you back and ultimately fail. These are damaging obstacles we have created, and a system of negative patterns that we put into practice to cope with stress, fear, vulnerability, and loneliness.

These barriers to freedom are not easy to identify because we have been practicing many of them for a long time. They feel ingrained within us, almost a part of us, and when we try to stop negative behavior—actions that damage our reputation, or thoughts that destroy our positive well-being—it is natural we are met with strong resistance.

Our goal is to break through this resistance and confront negative feelings and self-defeating mindsets creating havoc in our lives. Many of these emotions feel so natural that we are tapped into them without any awareness. Recognizing these barriers is the first step toward eliminating them and taking away their power.

Nothing has power over you unless you give it permission to. Are you giving your character defects permission to ruin your life? Your answer might be no, but when we look deeply at the truth of our current situations and the patterns keeping us there, we see the everyday decisions made, almost unconsciously and out of repetitive habit, that keep us spinning within a negative cycle.

These barriers allow us to avoid taking responsibility for the situations in our own lives. We practice avoidance tactics, pass the blame, complain about our problems instead of solving them, and embrace the false belief that we're no good.

The Obstacles Holding You Back

Here is a list of six barriers that could be holding you back. We will discuss these throughout the book, but for now, take notes and think about the barriers that apply to your life.

Barrier 1: You are blaming someone [or something] for your loss in life while holding on to resentment.

Blame is a major obstacle that prevents you from growing and blinds us to the reality of the situation. Blame creates negative energy that focuses on anger while building on resentment. While we feel entitled to hold our grudges and accuse others of mistreating, abusing, or disappointing us, we are fueling the pain by hanging on.

You will never be free as long as you're holding someone else accountable for your setbacks.

There were times in your life when others may have harmed you. As a child, you might have been critiqued or devalued and now, years or decades later, you are still recreating these hurtful feelings. We blame our parents, friends who rejected us, or people we trusted who betrayed that trust.

When we blame people for the negative stuff in our lives, we cannot take responsibility for it. You are throwing out a lot of negative vibrations when you carry resentment around expecting an apology.

Bitter complaining, playing the victim, or wishing the people who rejected you and created these feelings of shame would somehow show up and apologize for their behavior is not realistic. You may never get that recognition, apology, or show of appreciation that you are expecting.

We need to take control of this obstacle by owning responsibility—not for what happened, but for what you're doing about it now. It takes a strong will to recognize that by latching on to the past, we bring it forward into the future.

We will look at blame more in the upcoming chapter, as it is a powerful roadblock that needs to be addressed.

Action Task

Write down the name of one person you are resenting at the moment. Then, write down three reasons why you resent this person. What benefits are you reaping by holding on to your blame? Do you think there is someone in your life who holds a grudge against you? If so, why?

Action Task

For the next 24 hours, think of nothing but the positive traits of the person you are blaming. If you can't come up with one, try to visualize the life of this person and at least one difficulty they are dealing with. Did this person have a hard life? Were they born in poverty or have they been the subject of bullying?

If you can't think of anything positive about them, it's important to consider where they might be coming from. Again, this does not excuse their behavior if they wronged you. It's not about that. The purpose of this is to heal your negative emotions by owning them.

Barrier 2: You have tried to change before, and it didn't work.

If you have ever tried to break a bad habit, you know it isn't easy. You had to keep trying. If you gave up after the first or second attempt, you'd fail. We know that changing a pattern or a bad habit isn't easy. It takes persistence and diligence. But too often we give up after a few attempts, and then we say, "There, you see? I knew it wouldn't work out." But it can work out, if you stick with it.

Throwing in the towel only guarantees that you'll stay stuck where you are.

Think of a time when you failed to reverse a habit or stop a negative pattern. Was it an addiction? Do you remember why you weren't successful? If you succeeded in changing it, what did you do differently? When it comes to relaunching your life, we have to commit to breaking the patterns that are setting us up for repetitive failure.

Sometimes we try to change and then give up and move on when we don't get the results we want. This cycle repeats itself until we have exhausted all attempts.

Action Task

Consider a time in your life when you tried to learn something new. How long did it take you? Did you give up when you made a mistake? If you have become proficient at anything in your life, chances are you kept working at it until you were successful. We've all given up on something because we lost interest or we decided it no longer mattered.

Now, identify something you tried that *did* work and why. Why were you successful? What did you do that made the process easy?

When I am trying to change a behavior pattern or habit, I break it down into small steps. The "baby steps" method works best. Instead of trying to change everything at once, focus on just one thing to begin with.

For example, let's say you want to build up courage to become a public speaker. If you have a fear of public speaking, going before an audience of 500 would be too much for you. So, start small.

You could do a Facebook Live event. Or, watch the presentations of public speaking masters **Tony Robbins**, **Les Brown** and **Kyle Cease**. Model the way they speak and move. You can practice this alone or in front of a mirror, and then try it in front of a small group of friends.

Barrier 3: You tried to make these changes alone without reaching out for help.

Often, we'd rather try to change by ourselves in order to avoid becoming too intimate with others. We feel more secure and safe when isolated because there's less to lose.

Many people spend years trying to change something alone and with little success. I know I did. But it wasn't until I admitted I needed help that I was able to move through the real pain points.

You don't have to do it alone. You can find a mentor or a guide, join an online forum, or connect with people who can help you through local support groups. Overcoming obstacles and handling fear is best done when in the company of people who have been there themselves. They can offer support, guidance, and communicate your feelings in an atmosphere and relationship of trust.

Action Task

Find a mentor, connect with an accountability partner, or hire a therapist. I would recommend an online presence as well as meeting up in person. Try to connect with a support group that has weekly or monthly meet-ups in your area. Join an online group for support. Reach out for help from members you connect with.

Barrier 4: At your very core, you believe that you are unlovable, unwanted, and that everyone you meet will reject you.

These beliefs keep us paralyzed with fear. We continue to repeat the same internal monologue. Our habits remain the same. Behaviors are stuck and patterns stay in place for years.

For example, Bill felt paralyzed when his girlfriend and soon-to-be wife criticized him in public and made him feel small. But he tolerated this because he didn't feel deserving of anything better.

For him, it was a familiar feeling because it connected him to his childhood when his mother did the same thing. With therapy, he was able to see this pattern and leave the relationship. Bill was attracted to women who exercised emotional power over him, even though it made him weak and fearful.

Action Task

Become a self-observer. When you feel anxiety, fear, or the sense that you're being devalued, what is the situation? Is it when you are in a relationship? During an argument? When someone is criticizing you? By marking the situation, you can find out what's triggering your fear.

By observing how you behave in relationships, either at work or in private, you can identify the negative emotions that are trapping you. Throughout this book, we will target the specific negative emotions and how to deal with them.

Action Task

Make a list of your closest friends and the people who love you the most. Then, for each of them, list why you think they're in your life. What character traits do you have that attracts these people to you? Doing this simple exercise puts the truth (and the lies) into perspective.

Barrier 5: You are hooked into escape strategies that have proven reliable.

Over the years, we build our favorite strategies for escapism. You have your own devices that work for you. Your internal addictions are connected to the patterns of defeat that have defined you.

Escaping from reality is a coping mechanism that we develop as a defense to deal with internal pain. Escape feels natural, adding relief to an otherwise stressful situation.

For example, you might avoid going to social gatherings because you don't want to engage in conversation with others. You believe they will see you as strange or different. You avoid social exclusion through isolation. This is your escape pattern.

You might use other devices to numb you so that you won't feel anything, such as drinking, binge eating, or watching hours of TV so you can switch your mind off.

Our escape tactics are designed to keep the negative patterns active. They are reliable because they are effective. When we distract ourselves, we don't have to face the reality of our situation. We go through life reacting, escaping, and never healing from within.

Our beliefs are powerful indicators of who we think we are. The strength of these beliefs has everything to do with your success at building better avenues of self-esteem and confidence. But don't worry. You don't have to change everything at once. This is a journey and not a race. It's a program and not a test. You can't fail, even if you keep slipping back.

You must commit to the desire to move forward, push through the walls of resistance, and recognize that much of what you've invested in has been a fallacy. Most likely, the bad stuff you believe about yourself isn't true.

So, you've done things you're not proud of? Show me someone who hasn't. Knowing that we can move beyond emotional pain and set up a life—a new way of living—without holding on to all the negativity is a path I hope you are willing to take.

We will cover the escape routes we use in the upcoming chapter.

Action Task

Write down the methods you identified as your core escape strategies. When your escape patterns are triggered, what do you feel at the moment? Is it loneliness? Boredom? Anxiety? Your escape strategy is connected to your past experiences.

Action Task

Looking ahead, how do you see your life unfolding if you continue to use escape as a coping mechanism? Do you see the life you want or the life you have defaulted to because you continued to escape from reality?

Barrier 6: You are inconsistent with intentional actions.

In habit development, the only habits that are eventually successful are the ones you practice on a consistent basis. If you approach change with an "I'll do it when I feel like it" attitude, you'll never get around to it. We accomplish nothing when we lack commitment.

As we move through the material in this book, you will be challenged to look at the one person you have been avoiding: **Yourself**. When it comes to dealing with life experiences related to rejection, failure, defectiveness, and low self-esteem, realize and recognize the escape routes you've been using to avoid looking within. The key to making progress is sticking with consistent patterns of intentional actions.

Action Task

What do you do consistently every day? This can be anything from journal writing to brushing your teeth. You will notice the actions you do every day are the things you do well. We can use this when we recover from our negative emotions.

For example, reading a positive mantra or quote first thing in the morning for ten minutes can mean the difference between a good day and a day of destructive thoughts leading to depression. Find a positive action, just a small one that you can practice to start moving from that place of fear toward freedom.

Creating Better Solutions

This is a book of action. In the coming chapters, we will take a look at negative mindsets and emotions that may be holding you back, as well as the strategies for breaking free and recovering. Nothing is permanent. You can recover and create a better lifestyle than the one you have now. Even if you're living a great life today, we can still take it up a notch.

For every failure, we can make a comeback. For every rejection, we can discover something better for ourselves. When feeling low in confidence, we can tap in to that internal powerhouse of positive energy and learn to thrive.

CHAPTER 2

Justifying the Evidence: Are You Good Enough?

> *"To establish true self-esteem, we must concentrate on our successes and forget about the failures and the negatives in our lives."*
>
> — **Denis Waitley**

Why do we lack self-esteem? Where do these feelings of defectiveness originate? Why do I have this underlying anxiety and fear of vulnerability when engaged in conversation? How is it I am always thinking everyone I meet is better than me, and I can't measure up? Why do I feel different?

In this chapter, let's take a look at the logical reasoning as to why we see ourselves as people who are just not good enough. Take a moment to think back to when you were a child. Did you always have these feelings? Were you always lacking confidence, or held back by fear?

As children, we are fearless in so many ways. But as the years pass by and we discover ourselves through experiences, a transformation takes place. Some people push up and beyond their potential. They appear strong, willful and prepared to take on the world, expressing their maximum potential.

Does this mean we are any less successful if we struggle? I don't think so. The struggle is the journey. But it can defeat many of us if we lack the know-how to deal with life's difficulties. You may have been raised in a critical, negative environment. Years later, you might be carrying many of the traits you learned, and they may have morphed into a series of negative patterns that have become self-destructive.

What does it mean to be self-destructive? For many, it is about struggling with addiction. Others engage in escape tactics and self-defeating behaviors that hinder growth and stop positive progress. Any behavior that effectively damages your self-esteem, kills your confidence, and adds to your misery is a self-defeating pattern. And these are difficult life patterns to quit.

If you are reading this book, chances are it is because you struggle with one or more negative patterns. These patterns could be causing you to act out destructively from a very mild case to more extreme situations.

Many people feel that they were born different, somehow. Incomplete. Flawed. Because of this, we have created a system of behaviors for ourselves that help us cope. Many of these coping mechanisms may deal with addiction and substance abuse. Other negative habits may include compulsive spending, overeating, or fear-driven behaviors that result in destructive outcomes.

Many issues relating to rejection, perfection, or self-esteem can be traced back to childhood. The child might've felt abandoned, devalued, or was perhaps held to such high expectations that the fear of failure was imminent.

Those we trusted didn't always come through for us. You may have been criticized heavily by your parents, belittled, or ignored altogether in favor of a brother or sister. This has left most of us with emotional scarring. These are things we can't forget, or have tried to bury, but we've been unsuccessful.

Someone once said to me, "You have to switch the lenses you are looking through. They're broken and outdated. When life isn't working in your favor, it is time to change the view. You have the power to change it."

The first step you must take is an analysis of where you are now. Let's examine the evidence against yourself. Think of this as a court case, and you are representing yourself. To start with, here are some examples of what we might call "evidence" that seems to prove a lack of worth. Check off the items below that you can relate to:

- I am not as successful as most people I meet.
- Everyone I know is married and has a good job, and I don't have either of these things.
- I don't measure up to everyone around me.

- I feel overwhelmed by how hard I push myself. I just want to succeed, but all my successes don't matter because I'm soon chasing the next one.
- There isn't any stability in my life.
- I feel like everyone is "better" or "above" me in some way.
- I keep thinking something bad is going to happen to me.
- People have always let me down. How can I trust them?
- When I was growing up, my father told me I was never "good enough."
- When I get involved with people, I feel like I'm completely vulnerable.
- I've been rejected most of my life.
- I've been told I'm boring. I never have anything interesting to say. I can't even form an opinion about something.
- My whole life I've been on the outside looking in.
- Growing up, my family was highly dysfunctional. I always tried to hide how different we were from other families.
- I am always worried about my appearance around others—my weight, my looks, my height. It makes me very self-conscious.
- I showed up at a party once and didn't talk to anyone. I just sat there watching the crowd have fun. It's like they were rejecting me.

- I don't love myself very much. I have a negative self-image.

Can you relate to some of the statements above? We all have issues to varying degrees regarding self-worth, as well as the emotions and feelings we go through when involved in social, personal, and business relations. These are deep emotional feelings of failure, rejection, and low confidence. Many people deal with these problems every day. To cope, we have created our own survival mechanisms, a defense barrier to protect ourselves from pain.

But these defenses are walls that keep us trapped. They do very little to make the problems go away. Instead, an actionable program is needed to move you away from dysfunction and into a better, healthier state in which you measure up, participate, and are able to approach anyone or anything with the confidence that, yes, you are good enough.

We need to instill within ourselves the belief that we are good enough.

But first, let's kill the negative illusions that tell lies about who you are. Here is a list of the lies we tell ourselves:

- I'm worthless.
- I'm no good.
- I'm flawed.
- Compared to others, I just don't have what it takes.
- I'm dull and boring.
- I'm constantly being rejected.
- I'm not that attractive.
- I'm just not that smart.

- I'm a failure at everything I do.
- I'm too different from others to be accepted.
- I've never been liked. I never will be.
- I'm better off alone.

These are the mental programs we have constructed over the years, and they have taken over the way we think, act, and behave. They are killing our way of life. They have distorted reality as we know it.

Our goal is to throw these old, worn-out beliefs away. Starting today, you are taking a new path and a better direction in your life. Creating a new reality. Building different bridges. You are relaunching the way you think, behave, and act.

The evidence you have used to prove you are not good enough is convincing. There are hundreds of examples we can use to show the world why we don't matter, why nobody cares, and the excuses that are validated to settle our case. The failures you've had, the people who have criticized you, or the relationships that never worked out.

What if I told you that the self-image you have built for yourself has largely been influenced by the opinions and ideas of false critics who know nothing about you? Would you believe me?

I am talking about your parents, peers, teachers, and relationships from your past. But most of all, I am talking about you.

It doesn't matter what you have been led to believe about yourself. If you failed in school, so what? Perhaps your high school sweetheart left you for someone else after graduating, and you still feel vulnerable. Okay, now what? Maybe you work in a job you hate because you were told by the employment center that you had no skills to offer. Really?

You are not alone. We all experience failures, but this doesn't mean we are failures.

We are keeping ourselves down and, here is the real shocker, nobody else is responsible for the way your life is transforming except you. Here's the first thing we are going to set straight:

You are the **Master Gardener** of your own life. You are responsible for your failures and your successes. You don't always have control over the outcome or results, but what you can control are your actions and how you respond to the outcome.

You have the personal power to create change at any given moment. If you are waiting for someone else to show up and do it for you, good luck. You'll be waiting a very long time. Nobody cares about how you feel, but you can create a self-image of yourself that is strong, built on resilience, and you'll no longer need anybody for validation, confidence, or permission.

As children, we needed these things very much. But we didn't get all the encouragement, love, or acceptance that we should have. We still hurt from the loss of missing out on this, and while we can't reinvent the past, we can recover from it in time.

From today forward, you have permission to be good enough. This is where the change starts.

Justifying the Evidence

When it comes to being good enough, low self-esteem and a lack of confidence play a large part, but these are only symptoms of the condition, and not the condition itself. You can boost your confidence but still feel uncomfortable in your own shoes. In many cases, confidence is dependent on the situation you find yourself in. We have to look beyond the symptoms and tackle the primary source.

It begins with your self-image. The beliefs, values, and thoughts you have about yourself are important. You are only as good as the thoughts that feed your mind.

When we have a weak self-image, this is supported even further by the evidence that we have built up against ourselves to prove or justify our sense of worth.

Growing up, Sarah struggled with her physical appearance. She was overweight as a child and was teased terribly in school. She went on diets, stopped eating, and even lost most of the extra weight. She was no longer overweight, but she still held on to the self-image of the "poor little fat girl" who was bullied in school.

People may think highly of you, but if you cannot see yourself as good enough, what others think won't matter. You'll always react to the world or respond to it from your own sense of self-worth. The opposite is true as well. A crowd of people could be against you and yet, you are unbroken by their criticism. The bottom line is, we cannot and should not rely on the opinions of the external world.

A friend of ours, named **George**, said this about forming a self-image:

> *I was always changing my skin to meet the agreement of my environment. If someone liked me for something I did or said, I would do more of it to keep getting praise. I feared being disliked, so I tried hard to do what people expected. I would agree, even if I really didn't, and commit to doing favors for people, even if I didn't want to do something. If they liked me, it would feed the ego of my self-image. If they didn't like me, I would feel worthless and devalued.*

This is a good example of how we try to fit in to society, to play by their rules and do as they say to avoid being rejected or ostracized.

We will be working on our self-image. But keep in mind, this will take a lot of work. There are no easy shortcuts. But you can begin by taking a small step forward. You can start right now with a simple decision.

From this moment on, you are focused on changing the behaviors that have held you back from becoming all that you can be. From today forward, you are rejecting the negative voices in your mind and choosing to adopt positive change.

Remember, we have years of so-called "evidence" that we feel justifies our worthlessness. However, this evidence is not real. It is made up of years of false beliefs, and our goal is to shift your perspective and paint your life on a new canvas.

Many of our negative perceptions originated in childhood. We learned them from our parents, teachers, and friends, as well as from our experiences.

My friend **Dennis** said this about his childhood:

> *Growing up, I was always trying to please my parents. I tried hard at school, joined sports, even learned to play piano for a while because I thought it would make my father appreciate how hard I was working. I even won a competition once. But it didn't matter. They were both preoccupied with their own lives, and the only time they recognized anything is when I did it wrong. Then I never heard the end of it. And as for the competition I won, they never showed up.*

In Dennis's case, he felt abandoned by the people who were supposed to love him the most. He then spent most of his life in pursuit of success that was never recognized. At least, not by him. Others could see his achievements and how much potential he had, but Dennis had a relentless hunger that could never be satisfied. No matter what he did or how much he earned, it wasn't enough.

He never had an existence that was good enough. Not until he decided that he was finished trying to please others. When he made that choice to no longer care what people said or what they thought, and when he decided that only he could determine his sense of self-worth, things changed. He moved into a different playing field.

Looking back over our lives, each of us can pull apart the moments when our emotions and feelings were stepped on, struck down, and we were made to think we were nothing. You may have been in an abusive relationship or treated poorly by those closest to you.

But we are not going to jump on the pity train. Yes, we will identify the experiences that shaped our fractured image, but then we'll throw aside these painful memories and rebuild.

CHAPTER 3

The End of the Blame Game

"People may flatter themselves just as much by thinking that their faults are always present to other people's minds, as if they believe that the world is always contemplating their individual charms and virtues."

— Elizabeth Gaskel

The blame cycle is a powerful trap. As we deal with emotional hurts, we seek to escape pain. We blame the people who made us feel less-than.

- The overly critical parent who didn't support you.
- The lover who abandoned you.
- The people who bullied and teased you.
- The partner who cheated on you.
- The teacher who told you, "You're no good. Why don't you quit this class?" (This is true. It happened to me.)

All of these things lead back to creating a victim mentality. Life can be difficult and it isn't always fair. Not everyone has been kind. Maybe your parents could have loved you more. Teachers may have ignored you because they pegged you as the kid who would never make it. You were ousted and made to feel different.

On the other hand, maybe you were an overachiever. You had a lot of pressure from family and competition to stay ahead in grades, sports, or something else. You constantly lived with the fear of failing. You were taught that winning was everything and so you never had a chance to be yourself, to enjoy who you are, or to explore your true potential.

When something triggers a negative emotion attached to the pain of our past, we switch over to survival mode. We want to evade, attack, or defend. Primarily what we want is to escape, and to do this we place blame on the other person.

We say things like:

"It is her fault I am this way."

"I didn't ask for any of this."

"If I were worthy, I would have been treated better. I guess I'm worthless after all."

Our pain is linked to some powerful internal dialogue that we have been practicing for a long time. It seems so natural that when we are triggered to feel our emotional pain, escape is the most natural way to handle it.

Blaming people, places, and things for your misfortune is like waging a silent war on all the people who did you wrong: the parents who mistreated you, the relationships that abandoned you, or the boss who fired you. This is not a perfect world, but you can create a better one for yourself. You can reclaim your power by putting an end to blame.

When we decide we're responsible for everything that happens in our lives, this is the first step toward regaining personal power. It isn't about what's been done to you. It's about how you perceive the circumstances you're presented with.

On the other side, **you** accept total responsibility for the experiences in your life. You claim them and make a firm decision right now that everything that happens to you is a direct result of your actions. It has nothing to do with past events.

When you hold on to the pain of the past and point the finger at others because of the way things turned out, you're the only one who ends up suffering. You give up your right to make this life an amazing journey. Instead, it becomes a pathway to deeper suffering. If it is fulfillment, peace, and serenity you are after, then make a decision to move forward and claim your right to be free.

Blame keeps you trapped. Acceptance moves you forward and you become powerful, resilient, and independent. Instead of feeling vulnerable, trapped, and powerless, you are free to choose and feel confident.

But letting go of this blame isn't the same as forgiveness. First of all, you don't have to forgive anyone for anything. Unless you want to. And to be honest, many people have had things happen to them that are unforgivable. Letting go of blame doesn't mean excusing people, either, or saying, "That's okay. You did what you did. I'll get over it."

You Have a Choice

Denis Waitley, a motivational speaker and bestselling author, once said, "There are two primary choices in life: to accept conditions as they exist or accept the responsibility for changing them."

Reclaiming your **personal power** is about gaining power over yourself and has nothing to do with other people. The same can be said for forgiveness. If you decide the best way to move on is to forgive, it isn't to make the other person feel good. It's for *you*. If forgiving the people who hurt you is the only way you can recover, and end negative behavior patterns, then it's important to do so.

You need to think outside the box and push yourself beyond the negative feelings of inadequacy, shame, guilt, vulnerability, and failure. We will get into these topics more in the coming chapters. But just recognizing that they exist makes you more aware of when you are being internally "invaded."

Someone once said to me, "Change isn't easy. There is always a level of sacrifice we need to make to transform. And most people are not ready to sacrifice what they must in order to make that shift."

Transforming, reinventing or drastically shifting your life takes courage, commitment, and resilience. You have to act with intention. Without knowing why you are changing, you'll slip back into the negativity that keeps you there. To break free, you have to be committed to the process of changing your internal wiring.

Think of it this way: Growing up, we were exposed to a lot we didn't ask for. Criticism, emotional abuse, or neglect wired us for failure. But this doesn't mean we are failures. Far from it. You heal the parts of yourself that are damaged and you learn to build again.

So, if rock bottom is where you are, then that's where you begin. But you have to start somewhere. We all have our personal stories of success and failures, pain and happiness. If you are reading this book, chances are you're interested in having more happiness than pain. I can relate to that.

The biggest changes in my life happened when I made a decision to stop sabotaging my life and I was tired of feeling no good. When you walk around just living by default, it's really no life at all. You end up doing the things you don't want to do and spending your life engaging with people you don't want to be around.

The reason people stay trapped is because they try to defeat all of these things at once. They get overwhelmed and flooded with anxiety. This triggers an escape mechanism and you take immediate action on a self-defeating activity that feeds in to the negative cycle.

Recovery Action Steps

1. Identify your pain points.

Try to identify the ways you blame others for what you are going through. What escape strategies do you use that prevent you from facing the truth? Our escape strategies are like our own hidden passageways. What escape strategy are you employing?

Then, consider who you might be blaming. Is it a parent or a guardian? Someone else you trusted who betrayed you? Make a list of the people, places, and circumstances you hold accountable.

2. Visualize confronting the pain.

This is a visualization exercise. Think about and visualize the person who made you feel ashamed and worthless. See yourself getting angry, fighting back, and rejecting any form of harsh criticism. This can be a painfully emotional step. If the exercise is too intense, you may need to ask for support from a friend or seek professional help.

You might feel a lot of emotional pain in this step, such as anger, shame or embarrassment. There is nothing wrong with that. We are dealing with a lot of repressed emotions.

By repressing emotions and convincing yourself that you're not important, an underlying anger begins to grow.

Over time, it can channel into rage. If you feel out of control, find a professional to help you work through it. You don't have to do this alone. I would recommend a support group. Working together with others and voicing your feelings is the path to healing.

3. Write a letter to someone you resent.

The origin of your blame has played a powerful role in your life. But now we can strip that power away piece by piece. Resentment is a strong sense of bitterness you have toward someone or something else that did you wrong. Often, it's the reason why people struggle with hate and letting go.

Resentment can be powerful, but only when we feed into it. If you are trapped in resentment, you can break the cycle. Start by writing a letter to the person who hurt you. You can word it anyway you want. Nobody is going to see it except you. You don't have to send this letter if you don't want to or you can't for some reason. The letter is for you.

Express your feelings and how you know now that what happened wasn't your fault but that you're ready to move on and let go. Again, this is working toward a solution for forgiveness, but it's not for the other person, only for yourself.

4. Focus on your strengths.

Blame, resentment, and anger will keep you stuck. When these emotions come up, try to recognize them right away and consider what you're thinking about in that moment.

Chances are you were thinking of someone you hold a grudge against. If so, you can use the tactics above to take away its power. As long as you are feeding into the negative thoughts and empowering yourself as a helpless victim, you cannot change. You'll always be struggling to feel good about yourself.

What are your strong points? Here are some examples: honesty, integrity, confidence, loyalty, discipline, and compassion. We beat ourselves up because we fail to recognize the good traits we have that others see in us. Identify your top five traits right now and write them down on paper. Hang them up somewhere.

5. Make a gratitude list.

This is where you find real power. What are you grateful for? Who in your life do you love? As soon as you feel that urge to strike out and get revenge, shift your thinking toward gratitude, in turn shifting yourself from helpless to empowered.

The cycle of blaming keeps us trapped in the pain. Because of that, we can never heal, and we continue to feel bad about ourselves. We are taking action through attacking our abusers, causing us to remain victims.

Blaming people, your situation, or the world creates a sense of helplessness. You are handing over your personal power and buying into the belief that somebody else is responsible for making you happy or unhappy.

6. Forgive the people you are blaming.

This is not an easy step. To be clear, you are not forgiving people so that it makes them feel better. You are doing it for yourself. You have to move on from the negative images and resentments holding you back.

When we cling to the people or things that have wronged us, we are holding on to the victim mentality. As long as we are convinced that we have been wronged and we want revenge, it will be difficult to move ahead.

Right now, make a list of three people you are willing to forgive. But remember, you're doing it so you can move on from the emotional pain.

CHAPTER 4

Escape Tactics and Confronting Your Reality

"Every person has free choice. Free to obey or disobey the Natural Laws. Your choice determines the consequences. Nobody ever did, or ever will, escape the consequences of his choices."

— Alfred A. Montepert

When we feel emotionally vulnerable, or there is the possibility of rejection or failure, we turn to an escape plan or avoidance tactics to protect our fragility. This is an internal coping mechanism that has been conditioned to respond to any immediate threats that come up.

What would be considered a threat? Is it the fear of rejection, vulnerability, or criticism? We could be avoiding the situations that bring up painful experiences from our past, and to avoid reliving this event, we seek to escape from it.

To a certain extent, everyone has avoidance issues they regularly practice. It is quite natural to put the credit card bill at the bottom of the pile so we don't have to see it. Or maybe the house is a mess and you have to clean it up, but you'd rather watch TV. We avoid the things we feel are painful, uncomfortable, or we simply don't feel like doing. This leads to a habit of procrastination that, in extreme cases, can cause major problems.

But how about other avoidance issues, such as looking at yourself in the mirror? Making eye contact with someone? Avoiding interacting with people? These avoidance practices take on a different role in our lives. We escape out of fear—to escape from shame, to avoid being rejected, and to numb feelings of worthlessness and feeling flawed and defective. We avoid and escape to cope with negative and fearful feelings we lack the ability to control.

In doing so, we stay connected with our self-defeating patterns. Over the long-term, these patterns become deeply embedded into our habits until we can no longer recognize the damage being done. There's a lack of fulfillment, broken relationships, and job opportunities never realized.

The more committed we are to escape, the less committed we can be to recovering from these lifestyle patterns and developing a healthier way of functioning.

The Power of Avoidance

For many years, I avoided life as much as I could. I had a difficult time facing reality. I wouldn't even answer the phone if it was a number I didn't know. I was always protecting myself from being attacked, criticized, or made to feel less-than by those around me.

But my avoidance issues created a new set of problems. Thinking I was escaping, I was actually building a strong defensive wall to fortify my emotions and lock up any chance of recovering from my fear and sense of self-rejection.

The lesson learned is that **avoiding our issues** creates bigger issues.

Ignoring our problems is a problem. When we fail to get equipped with the right tools to overcome negative behavior, we become like the carpenter showing up for work feeling powerless to do anything without the tools to get the job done. You can learn to use the tools you need. You can adopt the tactics and strategies you want.

You were not born defective. Self-defeating behavior is a system of learned behaviors we adopt from our parents, friends, peers, teachers, environment, and life experiences. How we interpret the messages is a determining factor in the coping style we adopt.

For example, there's nothing wrong with being vulnerable. It is necessary in order for our relationships to grow and to foster a level of trust with those in our lives. But if your vulnerability is taken advantage of, and you are hurt by opening up in a relationship or shut down when you offer your opinion, you'll react to it as though you're being burned the next time it happens.

When the world makes you feel like you are no good, you seek to escape from it.

You become conditioned to stop taking risks. And when we stop trying for fear of failing or being ashamed, the next phase is isolation. You'll become conditioned to avoid and escape from your vulnerability so that you don't have to go through that pain of failing, rejection, or loss of control.

There are many reasons we escape, but the core excuse is that we want to avoid experiencing that pain over and over. Through escaping, avoidance tactics, and making ourselves busy or distracted, we can stop facing the reality of our situation by repeating the conditions of childhood.

Understanding how escape strategies work is the key to stopping them. When you recognize the tactics you use to escape, you'll stop running. By standing your ground, you are saying yes to a better way of life. You can end the pattern of self-defeat, walk into a room or any social situation and feel confident, relaxed, and be sure of who you are. You can stand up in front of a crowd of people and feel completely vulnerable and be okay with that.

The top three strategies that I personally engage in are denial, complaining, and holding on to resentment.

When I am in denial, I give myself permission to avoid the situation. I'll argue and even condemn the opinion of someone else to prove that I am right. When I complain about someone, I am trying to put myself above that person. I've even said, "I'm glad I'm not like that." But by labeling and condemning others for their mistakes, you are making yourself weak.

This is a lifelong pattern that is difficult to correct if you fail to recognize it.

Resentment is another issue. Show me a happy person who is full of spite. By putting down others, we think we are making ourselves feel better. Admit it: If you complain or label another, don't you feel superior to them? Isn't there a moment of superiority that takes you away from your inferiority? But it doesn't last. Before you know it, you are back to feeling sad and depressed again.

The reason is clear: We can't feel good about ourselves by trying to rise up and over others. Our goal is to create a healthy system of positive patterns that removes your dependence on negative and self-defeating behaviors.

Take a look at the list of **escape and avoidance tactics** and see if any of these escape methods are among your personal tactics for escape. Go through the list and check off the ones you recognize. You may have some avoidance tactics, but you might not recognize them yet. Just note the ones you use. On a scale of 1 to 10, with 10 being the strongest, rate the escape strategy as to how often or how frequently you employ it. How dependent are you on this strategy?

For example, my avoidance for meeting new people is about 6, so it is moderately strong. But complaining is around 8, which means I engage in it strongly.

Right now, rate the escape strategies from 1 to 10.

- Isolating
- Counterattacking (defensiveness)
- Addictive behaviors and numbing the pain
- Blaming
- Criticizing others
- Denial
- Failure expectation
- Failing to take responsibility
- Avoiding meeting new people
- Avoiding responsibility
- Getting angry (tantrums)
- Being passive
- Sabotaging self/others
- Compulsive spending and behavior
- Excessive worrying

- Labeling

- Complaining

- Holding back feelings or opinions

- Comparisons

- Holding on to resentments

- Thinking negatively about someone

- Being obsessive about something

- Rationalizing

- Feeling fear and doing nothing about it

Methods of Escape

First of all, we know we use avoidance tactics to sabotage ourselves so we don't have to be responsible for our success or failure. But do you *want* to fail? If we look at ourselves without judgment or criticism, I believe it is safe to say that we want to succeed in our lives.

There are several tactics we use to practice avoiding what we don't want to deal with. You might procrastinate and put things off indefinitely or distract yourself with other tasks to avoid the things that require your attention. Escape is a means of sabotage. You can run, but you'll never recover. We can only get better if we stand our ground. Through seeking better solutions to facing our own demons, we discover a new way of living on the other side of that pain.

Years ago, when I first noticed my methods of escape, I could see the patterns I was practicing almost on a daily basis. I would avoid talking about difficult subjects such as relationship problems. My attitude was, "It will work itself out." But what really happened is, it was either handled by someone else or, not taken care of at all.

Problem avoidance is an escape from reality. It is a tactic for survival. Because we never learned to deal with our reality as children, we have developed our own methods of coping. It may not be healthy, but it creates a feeling of inner security, although it's false. We learned to survive the hard way because we had no choice.

Handling Distractions

It is no wonder many people today are stuck in situations they can't escape from. We have so many devices to keep ourselves entertained that it's inescapable. So, we're not going to focus on the distractions in your life because they're only symptoms of the problem. Instead, we are staying centered on the real problem: you.

As I explained earlier, one way we remain stuck and feeling worthless is by blaming everything else for our present condition. It is always somebody else's fault. The investment you made just failed. The relationship you banked on collapsed. The job you were supposed to get was awarded to someone else.

When it comes to the distractions we use to fill up the emptiness we have, it isn't the fact that we have distractions that's the problem. It is our choices and the decisions made to use the distraction for escape. We have to stop running so we can get better. I realize this will be hard, because you might feel like you've been running most of your life.

Often, devices distract us from pain—games, TV, social media, alcohol, pornography, or shopping. The list is endless. Everyone has at least one device that serves him or her well. You have to recognize it and put it to rest. Once you identify the one distraction keeping you from freedom, you can work on the others.

Without realizing, we keep using it, similar to the addict who returns to the drug of choice when life goes horribly wrong. It is an escape mechanism and its pull is powerful. What devices do you use to escape from reality? You most likely have at least one, and possibly a combination of several. But for now, we will focus on just one tactic.

You can recognize it when you're under stress, or when you feel rejected or someone has just criticized you. You might use your distraction as a way to numb or control your emotions. In many ways, distractions have become silent addictions we rely on to make things easier so we don't have to deal with the problem.

A woman I know named **Brenda** had this to say:

> *I'd get asked out by friends but always made an excuse as to why I couldn't go out. The truth is, I hated meeting people because I never thought*

they'd like me. I had to pretend to be interesting when I really wasn't. I had to show I was happy and together when I'd be falling apart. So, I'd lie and tell people I was busy. Then I'd stay home and watch TV or use the Internet. I did things that focused on isolation and distracted me from what was going on out there. I always thought that once they got to know me, they'd lose interest anyway and my lack of worth would be validated. So, I was always trying hard to prove I had worth.

Brenda's case is similar to many others. She fears the pressure of showing up and performing, so she has created a life of isolation to protect her emotions and vulnerability. But in the end, she is alone, which she feels is better than humiliation.

What are you doing to stay distracted and hide the truth? Do you have your favorite devices and do they work? Are you left with a bitter sense of disappointment in yourself?

Distorting the Truth

The advantage of avoidance is that, in the short-term, we don't have to confront the uncomfortable situations that scare us. We don't have to face the truth about our problems or admit how trapped we are.

Avoidance distorts the truth and throws a veil of secrecy over the life we are living. It is a lie but a good one that helps us cope. We can move through our lives without taking responsibility, admitting fault, or looking seriously at our flaws. The illusion covers the pain.

The negative side to this, and the one we have to pay attention to, is that we never change. We are stuck in this perpetual maze of doubt, uncertainty, fear, and self-loathing. On the surface, we know we're escaping, and this reinforces our feelings of failure and defectiveness. Running away from the situation is a survival technique, like escaping from a burning building.

While we know that avoiding our problems isn't going to make them go away, such as ignoring an abusive relationship or an addiction, by not acknowledging it we're striking a bargain with ourselves. You have accepted that you are a self-defeatist without hope. You are, in effect, giving up on getting better.

> We are escaping the painful reality of facing our emotions that have become painful sore spots. By staying stuck, we will never change, we will not move forward, and we will not get what we want.

This is why, from this point onward, I encourage you to take a look at the parts of your life that you're escaping from. Do you avoid social situations for fear of rejection? Do you avoid taking on challenges or confronting your fear? What is it that you don't like about yourself? Do you remember at what point in your life you set up your escape route? Did you model escape strategies from someone else?

Chances are, one or both of your parents were escape artists. They probably didn't realize it. This was passed down as the model of how things are handled. Your family could've avoided problems or not discussed them at all. You learned to stay quiet and just accept it. But now we know that we can do better, and we have the courage and the personal power to change what we want through intentional choices.

We can choose to create the situations we desire instead of constantly fleeing from the circumstances that make us feel powerless. You have control over the mechanisms that can change your life, such as decision-making, thought creation, and internal beliefs.

Strategies for Staying Grounded

1. Set up a "trigger" for when you feel you're trying to escape.

Asking yourself to be aware of your escape pattern is the first step to putting an end to it. We all have certain triggers that make us switch over to fight or flight. It could be a certain situation or person. Comparing yourself harshly to someone and minimizing the success, or lack of success, that you have could be your trigger.

When you are near someone who is higher in social status, has more money and success, and seems to have a better life, it is easy to compare ourselves to them. This is how we push our confidence and self-esteem lower than it should be, by thinking we're not good enough.

The trigger around these people is always the same. We start to tear ourselves down and curse the life we have for what we could have. This is a recipe for depression and building your feelings of inadequacy.

True, you might not have as much as most, but how much do you need? At what point would you be satisfied? Do you have a happiness bar you'd like to reach? We can identify and switch off our triggers by questioning the reality of the reasoning.

2. Identify the various ways you escape.

Some examples include avoidance, isolation, arguing, and denial. By identifying how we escape, we can be better equipped to stop it when it happens. For example, a friend of mine—we'll call him Jonathan— uses criticism as a tool to attack people before they can target him. At his workplace, he is often accused of not admitting his responsibility when mistakes are made.

Jonathan has a hard time admitting fault. When he is at fault, he rarely admits it and tries to put it on someone else. This created a serious barrier, dividing him from his colleagues. He uses blame and being critical of others as a means to cope with his low-esteem. If he admits he is wrong, he is admitting failure, and that is something he's very ashamed of.

We all have escape vices. Procrastination to avoid doing things we don't like, labeling to cover up our own defective feelings by looking at someone else's faults, or acting out with addictive behavior to hide from our true feelings. In practicing these self-defeating coping mechanisms, we only condition ourselves to rely on them more. You could be at the point where you are very dependent on your escape strategy. As a short-term painkiller, it helps you forget, escape, or become numb.

We can only change this if we know how we are using our escape methods to avoid responsibility or looking at our real problems. Throughout this book, we will examine strategies for dealing with each pain point.

3. Focus on one escape strategy at a time.

We can't get better overnight. This is not a one-size-fits-all program. Especially where self-esteem is concerned, because we invested many years in beating ourselves up.

We practiced negative patterns intensely for some time before mastering them, and it'll take time to swing a balance between where we want to be and where we are now. But you can't do everything at once. Slow and easy does it. Making a shift in any habit or pattern involves a steady and consistent push to make change happen.

4. Write out your feelings.

One of the more powerful strategies I discovered for initiating change was to write out or record the feelings I was experiencing. There are several ways you can do this. Journaling your experience is one way, and I found this to be very effective. You can set aside twenty minutes a day for this. Make it a habit by doing it at the same time each day.

I set aside twenty minutes in the evening to write in a journal. I made some notes of how I interacted with people, any fears I had, and most importantly, I noted whether I did anything differently to change the pattern of my self-defeating behaviors.

Remember, one core reason we feel shame or guilt is because we are trapped in the patterns of our destructive behaviors. The habit keeps the pattern active. Once you break that pattern, and continue to break it, you heal the shame and guilt you've been holding onto.

5. Voice record your feelings.

The other strategy is speaking aloud into a recorder. You can use the recording feature on your phone, tablet, or other software such as Dragon Dictation.

This is a fantastic strategy because it is like having a conversation with yourself. If this feels uncomfortable, it is because you are breaking in your ability for self-expression.

6. Ask someone to hold you accountable.

Ask your partner or a close friend to help you. Once you have identified the ways you escape from your vices, get them to hold you accountable. For example, if you are in the pattern of avoiding having conversations with people, your partner can point out the times when you are being aloof or making excuses as to why you can't.

You could do the same for each other. Make a commitment to point out at least one negative escape pattern each week. Then, at the end of the week, sit down and discuss it.

How did you use your escape tactic? For example, one of my escape strategies was to make excuses as to all the reasons why I couldn't do something. I had an excuse ready for everything. If I had to fill out a form but I couldn't, it was because I couldn't find a pen.

If I passed up an opportunity for something to make life better, like a new job that I would be happier in, there was a reason why I couldn't set up an interview. Your escape is what holds you back. It has nothing to do with anyone else or any other person, place, or thing.

Check in With a Weekly Review

At the end of the week, review your progress. What triggers did you notice? How did you try to escape this week? Is there anything you avoided doing? How will you make yourself more aware of it for next time?

You should refer back to the list in this chapter and pay particular attention to the escape and coping strategies that you ranked a 6 or higher. Chances are these are strong escape patterns that are keeping you stuck.

Now that we've covered the basics of self-defeating patterns, how we keep them active and the strategies used to escape, let's take a look at the four mindsets that make up the bulk of our internal barriers.

—Section 2—

The Self-Defeating Mindsets

"All forms of self-defeating behavior are unseen and unconscious, which is why their existence is denied."

— Vernon Howard

CHAPTER 5

The Struggle with
Self-Esteem

*"The most beautiful people we have known are those
who have known defeat, known suffering, known
struggle, known loss, and have found their way out of
the depths. These persons have an appreciation,
sensitivity, and an understanding of life that fills them
with compassions, gentleness, and a deep loving
concern. Beautiful people do not just happen."*

— Elizabeth Kubler-Ross

Self-esteem is the relationship you have with yourself,
your relationship with other people, and how you
feel in the company of others. It's your global sense of
self-worth, how you value yourself, and how you
express your sense of self-worth to the world.

Do you see yourself as a person who adds great value to
the lives of others? Or do you feel unimportant, as if
your opinion doesn't matter?

Depending on how you view your self-image, this is the foundation your self-esteem is built on.

When we suffer from a sense of worthlessness, we are holding on to the beliefs that we're defective, different, and flawed. We feel that our sense of self-worth isn't good enough for the world, and so we escape from the areas in which we feel vulnerable or rejected. This could be at home in family situations, at work, or in social settings.

A low self-esteem impacts nearly every area of your life and contributes to negative beliefs of failure and rejection. If we cannot value ourselves, we shouldn't expect the world to, either. Depending on the outside world to increase your personal value leads to disappointment.

Your sense of worth and happiness is developed from within, and no matter how much you try to obtain it with external validation, it will never be enough. You can't rely on anyone to give you what you're lacking in personal confidence.

This is an empowering realization. We have the ability to generate our own levels of self-esteem and positivity. It's important to have a strong support system in place—people with whom you can discuss your emotions and ideas.

It's up to you to be flexible and willing to implement these positive changes. There is no magic formula for building self-esteem. It simply involves becoming aware that you're a person of worth and that you really do matter. The rest is constructing a new belief system to support this. It is up to you to start that change and in Part III of this book, you will find the tools to help you on this journey.

Weak self-esteem is that deep-down feeling that you're not good enough for anyone. You feel *beneath* other people. No matter how hard you try to fit in, you can never match up to those who look better, have more, or are more talented. There's always someone who is better educated, comes from a better home, has won awards and achievements, or has the best-looking partner. And you, of course, could never have any of these things.

Why?

You don't believe you deserve it. At the core of these defective beliefs, one of the most damaging is that, not only are you **inferior** to the people you meet, you **don't deserve** nice things in life.

We start building painful beliefs like this one from childhood. Years of criticism, shame, lack of praise or emotional trauma has ingrained our false beliefs that we are incapable and incompetent. This is a debilitating condition constructed throughout the years.

Fortunately, it is not a permanent condition. We can reverse the effects and feel great about ourselves, no matter what the personal history books say. The key is to stick with the plan for recovery and never give up.

Many people feel inferior to others to a certain degree. And realistically speaking, there are people who have more, look better, are more charming, or went to better schools. But these are not the reasons we have low self-esteem.

People experience low self-esteem in different ways and in different situations. Most of us with low self-esteem are tapped in to the negative and defective sides of our character.

Every day we are being drip-fed doses of negativity in the form of internal monologue, self-sabotaging thoughts, and the voices of criticism from ghosts of the past. Most of the voices we are hearing aren't real; they are voices of those no longer with us, but we haven't learned to let go of them yet.

Here's something **Ted** shared:

> *In my work, I had to meet with lots of clients at these social functions. I hated it. These are people with degrees, connections, and high IQs—well, many of them thought so. I was supposed to mingle and make connections with these people, but I was terrified. I have always had this feeling deep in my gut that I didn't belong there, that they would find out I was a fake and I'd be humiliated once it was discovered I hadn't gone to a prestigious university. I can remember after these functions were finished, I'd literally run from these people, the social pressure right on my heels.*

Inferiority dysfunction has nothing to do with other people. We need to be clear about that. Ninety-five percent of what we are discussing in this book has very little to do with the opinions or attitudes of others. Rather, it has to do with how we interpret and assimilate information and allow it to control our thoughts and create negative beliefs.

There are certain beliefs and behaviors that keep us trapped for years and even decades, as our self-defeating attitudes and habits replay the same scenarios over and over again in our minds.

We replay the events that created our inferior personas. We listen to the voices of negativity and control as they feed mixed and false messages about who we are. We think this is just the way life is supposed to be.

The Traits of Low vs. High Esteem

These are the core traits of negative self-esteem. You can check any that apply to you. Then, we will look at the corresponding positives. I also included a general belief attached to each trait.

- Perfectionist attitude: I have to get this exactly right or they'll think I'm incompetent.
- Mistrusting others: What do they want from me?
- Blaming behavior: It wasn't my fault.
- Fear of taking risks: What if I fail and look stupid?
- Feelings of being unlovable: Nobody has ever loved me and nobody ever will.
- Dependence: Letting others make decisions for me.

- Fear of being ridiculed: I'm not getting up in front of those people to give a speech. And have them laugh when I get stuck on my words? No thanks.
- Self-critical: I am such an idiot. I'm just no good.
- General negativity and unhappiness: What's the point? It's hopeless.
- Refuses to accept positive feedback: They said that I did a good job, but it was just luck.
- Minimizes achievements or success: Anyone could have done this.
- Withdrawn from situations in which there could be rejection or criticism: I think I'll pass on that party invitation.
- Less persistent after failing or making a mistake: Well, I'll never do that again.
- Feeling unworthy becomes part of the identity: I'm a loser. It's just who I've always been.
- Limits our ability to view the world in a positive way.
- Creates a resistance to positivity: I just don't see anything good coming out of this situation.

Action Task

Now, for each of the traits above, consider how to turn them into a positive. This is a powerful exercise that will change your attitude almost instantly. It puts your negative self-image and beliefs under the scope. Turning a negative into a positive is like turning the car around after you've started down the wrong path. You decide to go the other way because you know it's the right path to follow.

For example:

Negative Illusion: *Minimizes achievements or success. "Anyone could have done this."*

Positive Reality: *"Yes, anyone could have, but they didn't. I did it. And if I had the chance to do it again, I could do even better the next time."*

Try this out for all of the above negative traits. Then, you'll learn to adapt this habit when you are hit with thoughts that put you down or minimize your worth and abilities.

Building an Identity

What we should identify with is what happens when our self-esteem is low. It isn't as recognizable as a physical injury, but if you have a low opinion of yourself, you are suffering from another kind of injury. It is internal and nobody should see that pain except you. If this goes untreated, you stand to spend much of your life walking around feeling unworthy, negative, depressed, and withdrawn.

In many cases, people who are depressed are running negative thoughts of themselves through their minds. There are other factors for depression, of course, but when it comes to the kind discussed in this book, we have to tag the negative thoughts, behavior, and attitudes that are killing our self-esteem so we can raise our confidence.

Negative thinking is a learned pattern. You were not born negative. It isn't an inherited trait. Negativity is a conditioned response. We learn to think and act this way. This is good news for us. It means we can retrain ourselves to think and act differently.

Patterns, habits, and behaviors can be reversed and changed completely. This is a lot of work and you have to dedicate yourself to sticking with your recovery. Whether it takes months or years, you'll change your mindset and ultimately your lifestyle.

Rise Above the Negativity

If you don't rise above it, you'll continue to stumble through life, holding on to the belief that you're unworthy. But that isn't true because the evidence isn't real. You can jack your esteem up in a matter of days.

How do we do that? Somewhere along the way, you were convinced that self-esteem was about the opinion of other people rather than your relationship to yourself.

The world will treat you according to how you treat yourself. The value you put on your own worth is the same value anyone else will. People who have strong self-esteem attract positivity. Not only attract it, but they also create it. In believing they are a person of worth, they show up to act the part. They can turn a frown into a smile and a negative situation into something worth remembering. How do we do this?

Intentional action. We act with the power of intention. You can do this in several ways. The first is the power of body language. The second is your intentional mindset. The third is making an intentional decision.

Your body language, the way you talk, your ability to make eye contact and how you carry yourself says everything about your confidence. Act the part and you'll become it.

The Self-Esteem Action Plan

It's time to fight back, and now you have enough ammunition to stand up and throw your own punches.

Here are six strategies I recommend you put into action right away. Don't wait for someone to give you permission to be yourself. You were never given permission before, and you don't need it now.

1. Draw the line.

When self-esteem is weak, we become accepting of the abuse others dish out, especially in close relationships. As children, we could only stand by while a parent criticized or devalued us. You may have continued to accept it because you believed you deserved it. As an adult, you still believe it. You still act small and are afraid to ask for what you want. Because of this, you open the door to becoming a target.

You might be in a relationship in which your partner is critical and condescending. If so, draw the line. You don't have to be harsh or angry. Tell them their behavior is no longer acceptable. It is not an easy thing to do.

When you assert your rights and take a stand, people who are used to seeing you a certain way—passive, internally fragile—might feel threatened by the new you. They might try to control you even more. This usually leads to the breakdown of the relationship. If so, it's best to end it. You don't have to be a punching bag.

Stand up.

Assert your expectations.

Reinforce them.

This is how personal power is regained and you're able to bring back the confidence that slipped away for such a long time.

2. Be aware of how you might be mistreating others.

In our days of feeling low, we might mistreat others just as we had been mistreated. We pass on what we know. An example would be someone who grows up in a home in which one of the parents is a tyrant. He or she then becomes the tyrant in relationships, targeting those who are willing to take it. The cycle repeats itself.

If you're on the other side of the fence, it may be your partner who points out your systematic bullying. Remember, we pass on what we know and bring everything we are into a relationship. From children to spouses to parents, nothing goes unnoticed. Just because somebody made us feel devalued doesn't mean we can do it to others. It won't heal our wounds. The cycle can only end with you.

Focus instead on praising those you care about. Practice gratitude for having them in your life. Catch yourself when you feel anger welling up inside you. Take time out and step away if you have to. Remember, we're dealing with fragile emotions.

3. Be aware of your feelings of shame.

We feel shame in positions of vulnerability. Growing up and lacking approval from the people who were closest to us is a painful reality. When we are detached from the pain of our past, it opens up wounds that we tried to bury through escape or avoidance.

Becoming aware of your shame takes courage. You have to be willing to step out of your shell of vulnerability. By exposing the lies that keep us scared, we can bring those feelings and memories to the surface.

If you could have a conversation with your younger self, what would you say? If you could visit the child who lost love and felt rejected, what would you say to her? How would you comfort her? Take ten minutes to imagine this. Were you compared to another sibling? Were high expectations placed upon you but you couldn't measure up? Think of a specific event and then see yourself acting differently. Imagine fighting back if someone criticized or belittled you.

4. Make a list of twenty qualities you like about yourself.

Here are some examples to get you started:

Do you hold the door open for people?

Do others say positive things about you?

Do you give 20 percent of your salary to charity?

Do you lend money to people if they need it?

Do you give up your seat on the bus?

Do you smile and greet people you don't know?

Do you have empathy for people who are struggling through a difficult time?

Are you a good friend? Husband? Wife? Considerate of others?

Dig deep and think about this. You might get stuck, but you can step away for a while and take a break. You can do this all at once or take a week to complete it. As you move through your day to day, you'll come up with more traits that you didn't realize were there.

The purpose here is to get you thinking of yourself in a positive way about who you really are. We need to start shifting our internal negativity into a more positive approach.

5. Make a list of the traits you would like to change about yourself.

What do you want to change? Are you too self-centered and need to focus on others more? Would you like to be more assertive? Do you complain too much? Do you procrastinate more than you should?

Building self-esteem takes time and effort, but you can make small changes every day. Simply do something for yourself, and then help someone else. When we give more of ourselves to others, it builds trust.

Stay focused on who you are. Don't let anyone treat you any less than you deserve. You are not always the problem. Follow the program here and you'll be creating a new sense of purpose when you are finally in charge of your own life.

6. Brainstorm Your questions.

You can write down your thoughts in a notebook. Now, look at the questions below and block in time to really think about your answers.

- How do you feel around authority figures?
- In what situations do you feel inferior?
- Is there someone in particular who makes you feel inferior? Has this person made you feel as if they're better than you, either by direct communication or through their attitude toward you? How do you feel these messages were conveyed?
- When you compare yourself to this person, in what ways does he or she seem smarter, more intelligent, or somehow more important than you?
- How could you become equal to this person? Is it something you feel you'd have to achieve or obtain?
- Do you try to be better than others so you can get ahead and start to measure up?
- Is there someone from your childhood who made you feel inferior through criticism or judgments. Was it a friend, a teacher, or a parent? What would you say to him or her if they were with you now?

264 • SCOTT ALLAN

- Imagine, for a moment, that he or she were standing in front of you right now. Start a conversation with this person. Ask this person questions such as: *What did you gain by acting this way? What do you hope to gain in the future if you continue to act this way?*

Even if you never see this person again, it is very empowering to have this "visual communication" and question the motives leading up to the criticism that impacted your self-esteem.

CHAPTER 6

Overcoming the Social Inferiority Mindset

"People tend to dwell more on negative things than on good things. So, the mind then becomes obsessed with negative things, with judgments, guilt and anxiety produced by thoughts about the future and so on."

— **Eckhart Tolle,** bestselling author of
A New Earth

In this chapter, we will look at the power of social inferiority and how we cope with our relationships with others and with ourselves as we learn to function proactively in social situations.

Social exclusion is about two different things. First, the relationships you have with others and how you interpret those relationships. Second, the relationship you have with your inner self and how you present yourself to people.

This is how you interact, communicate, and connect with the people around you—at home, in your community, and at work.

You could be stuck in the social anxiety mindset if you have these symptoms:

- I am always on the outside, looking in.

- I am alone, even when surrounded by others.

- Most people don't understand me. They don't want to be around me because I'm different.

- They are going to reject me because I am not at the same level. I am too unattractive, uneducated, and I have no social status.

- I always fumble with my words and say something stupid because I am so nervous.

- I have nothing to say to anybody. That's why I prefer noisy bars. You don't have to talk to anyone.

- I know others are judging me based on where I went to school, my job, or what my achievements are.

- I overcompensate for my deficiencies and lack of social skills.

Social situations are very difficult for many people if they are dealing with a lack of confidence, low self-esteem, or rejection issues. Some people avoid social situations altogether, while others feel exhausted after an hour and have to go home. When it comes to being around people, this is when the challenges arise that are linked to our feelings of inferiority.

Robert shared his feelings about this topic:

> *I always had this belief that I was below everyone. I have spent most of my life, as long as I can remember, trying to be good enough, to measure up so I could get to a point people that accepted me, but I never got there. Everywhere I went I had this feeling of inferiority, like I was born with less than everybody else. Then one day it occurred to me: It was me who was rejecting myself. The acceptance I was looking for from others had to come from me first. Once I recognized that, everything changed.*

A Case of Social Survival in Dubai

Several years ago, I attended a large three-day seminar in Dubai. Over two hundred people gathered in one large conference hall for a three-day workshop on Global Education. I have never done well in large crowds of people. Knowing that many of them would be highly educated professionals, including doctors and business executives from Fortune 500 companies, I was already feeling inferior before I arrived.

During the first day, I felt self-conscious, socially awkward, and different the whole time. I was trying to impress people and even lied about my 'achievements.' Sometimes we'll do anything to gain the approval of others.

For me, the real challenge came when participants were split into smaller groups. This was more terrifying than being part of the small tribe. Each group was given a small project, and we had to share our ideas on what it took to succeed. When I heard this, I froze. My feelings of rejection came flooding in.

What if they hate my ideas?

What if they realize I'm not as intelligent as they are?

What if they find out I'm a fraud?

My initial plan was to escape. I wanted it to be over. Several members in the team had already taken on a leading role while the rest of us joined in. I remained largely silent. After all, what did I have to contribute? Why did they need me, anyway?

Then, one of the ladies in the group turned to me and said, "Well, are you just going to stand there or do you have any ideas?"

It was a direct statement meant to put me on the spot. And it did. Every fear I'd ever had about social interactions was awakened. The other members, none of whom I knew, were now waiting for me to say something. I felt awkward and socially incapable of working in a group of strangers. I could only mutter one sentence: "Bathroom break!" And that was it. I was gone and nobody cared. They went on as planned, the project was completed, and I stayed in the bathroom until it was over.

Am I a social reject? I don't think so, but the problem wasn't with the people in the group. There was nothing wrong with anyone there, in fact. Everything I experienced had been created by me from an internal source. It was as if a door had been opened to my soul and everyone in that room had access to it.

During those three days, I realized I had issues with social exclusion, rejection, and a fear that I had never experienced before. Why?

Because I had spent most of my life avoiding it. On a subconscious level, we are aware of our weaknesses. You might have a fear of rejection, a fear of crowds, or maybe you just feel uncomfortable around people in general. If so, our course of action is to avoid the fears we don't want to face. This all comes back to childhood feelings and origins of inferiority.

I learned a lot of things about myself in those three days. I learned that I use escape as a means of avoiding contact with others. To avoid looking stupid or being ridiculed, I run. It's a natural instinct for those of us who are wired into our escape strategies.

A Case of Social Survival in Dubai: Part 2

There is one more side of the story. Fearing being in a group is one thing. There is the fear of failure, of being judged, or criticized in front of others. These are experiences you can probably relate to. But as the seminar was wrapping up, and I was feeling less anxious, the worst—or the best—part happened. I was seated at a table in the back, trying to avoid attention and blend in, when the final speaker stood to deliver the closing speech.

He started by passing the microphone around to the tables. At each table, we each had a number, and when the mic landed on the table, if your number was called out, you had to speak for one minute about how you were going to apply what you learned at the seminar back in the real world. When the mic landed at our table, my number was called. It was 47.

At first, I couldn't move. I had nothing to say because I had no speech prepared. But neither did anyone else and they seemed to do just fine. Every part of me was now tuned in to my greatest fear: public speaking. Now I had over two hundred pairs of eyes focused on me. I could literally feel my throat dry up and close. If you've experienced the feeling that comes with the fear of speaking in front of people, it can only be described as if your body and mind is shutting down. You can't think. In some cases, people lose the ability to speak.

Someone put the mic in my hand because it was still lying on the table. I got to my feet but it was as if the room was spinning. My social awkwardness, the fear of rejection, and all those feelings of inferiority were switched fully on. But then something else happened. In an instant I recalled a quote by Mark Twain. I had written it down days before to remind myself what the meaning of fear is:

Courage is resistance to fear, mastery of fear, not absence of fear.

— Mark Twain

Up until this point, I had always avoided the things I was afraid of. I didn't want anything to do with people or challenges. I would keep fear at a distance, tucked away in a corner where it couldn't get out. But the problem with this is, we never grow when we stay hidden. We never learn or develop or reach our full potential. We stay the same, and I wanted to be different.

So, I spoke for around ten minutes. To this day, I don't remember what I said. What I do remember is that, in a moment of doing it scared, I was able to defeat the one fear that I had always avoided.

The main point to the story is, so can you. When we believe we are "worthless" and "inferior," these are only lies. Holding on to these beliefs is what makes us fail. If you are tired of failing and running away, now is the time to seize the day and make a change.

Breaking the Chain of Social Inferiority

The social rejection mindset is never about the other person. It is about you. Other people can do and say things that might cause us to feel inferior, but in the end, we decide how to interpret the situation.

Robin shared the following:

> I was never good at meeting people. I just hated it from the moment we had to say 'Nice to meet you.' Right away there was this sense of anxiety as if I

had to show this person that I was as smart, as functional, as ambitious as they were. Sometimes I'd say nothing and people would just start talking about themselves, about their lives and achievements and their dreams and ambitions. These were the best encounters because I never had to say anything. I didn't want them to know anything about me.

People who struggle with social situations are dealing with conflicting fears and anxieties. An underlying doubt tells them they won't measure up and that in order to be accepted, they must prove their worth. This is done through bragging about achievements or discussing ambitions and goals.

If you have rejection issues, you may feel completely vulnerable. You have an underlying fear that somebody will find out that you're a fake and announce it to the crowd.

You feel defective, alone, and isolated but you're the only one who knows this. So you put on an act. You try to be one of those people. You might even talk loudly or try to get attention just to appear like you're a socialite. But inside, you have a crushing feeling that you might be discovered.

No matter what, you feel less-than other people. Everyone else seems to have better jobs, better clothes, and a better education. They're funny and witty, bringing life to the party, and you feel dull and boring, as though you have little to contribute.

These thoughts bring on self-criticism. You can't stand to be near others because you don't want to be seen as someone who is dysfunctional or different. This can be traced back to our earlier childhood memories.

Susan shares her story here:

> *I was always different as a kid. I wasn't good at sports or even school. I would watch all the popular kids get attention, win awards for academic achievement or be accepted. I was always on the outside looking in, like having my face pressed up against the glass and watching the party happening from the outside, but I was too afraid to go in. If I did, I'm sure they'd reject me.*

The symptoms of feeling less-than are different for everyone, and we all have a story to tell regarding how we came to think so little of ourselves. You may feel insecure, inferior, defective, damaged, or completely detached from the rest of the world, but I want you to know one thing: It's okay.

You can accept yourself as you are, and in realizing that you're just like everyone else, try to do the best you can with what you have. This takes the pressure off constantly feeling as if you have to measure up.

If you feel like you must prove your worth to someone just to get them to accept you, consider walking away from that person and taking a break. This individual might be expressing his or her own expectations. Perhaps they expect people to challenge themselves to measure up. You don't have to do that. You can be yourself, and you'll attract people who will appreciate you for who you are. Those who don't will find another group to latch on to.

Unrealistic Standards and Perfection

David was brought up in an emotionally deprived family. The dysfunction began at an early age. Everything he succeeded at was never good enough, and his mother, who was a perfectionist and rarely showed emotion, never praised his accomplishments.

David said:

> *One day I came home from school with my report card. I had an average of 77, which was the best I'd ever done. But when I showed it to my mother, she said, 'Where'd the other 23 points go?'*

Due to this, he continually strived for perfection. The problem with trying to be perfect is that you never reach your goals. You hit one milestone, and then you focus on the next one, which is even higher.

Always looking to outdo your past performance, you fail to celebrate victories in the moment. This creates a life lacking in fulfillment and leads to the pursuit of relentless achievements that are never praised. You are always trying to reach a pinnacle of success that you never arrive at.

The worst part about perfection is that perfectionistic people view failure as a devastating setback. Instead of learning from it and recognizing that failure is also a necessary part of success, we scold, put down and push ourselves harder.

The basic assumption is that failure is unacceptable. It is the classic all-or-nothing attitude and a crippling mindset. You are happy momentarily when you get a win, but you tear yourself apart when you suffer a loss. And losing is a big part of winning.

How can you appreciate a victory if you've never experienced a loss? The pursuit of perfection is a lie, and it always has been. Am I suggesting that we shouldn't do the best we can and achieve the highest pinnacle of our potential? Of course not.

Do your best, learn from what doesn't work, and make changes along the way. Keep adjusting. Instead of shooting for the top of some gigantic achievement, focus on the next rung of the ladder. How many people do you know who can leap from the bottom rung to the top in a single bound? It's one step at a time.

Trying to "act" perfect is a survival mechanism, too.

For example, Betty feels anxious in social interactions. She has a fear of not fitting in and tries to impress people to get them to like her. Because she never feels good enough for anybody, she has created a perfect persona for herself.

She rehearses at home before going out so that she knows exactly what to say to someone when they ask about her career or personal life. But it's just an act, and when the social event is over, she is exhausted.

Social Inferiority is closely linked with the perfectionist persona; we feel anxious because we have a secret we don't want anyone to discover. By hiding the worst parts of ourselves, we can conceal our true identity with a false one that appears normal in every way.

But it goes without saying that you can fool people for a little while, but sooner or later, you get trapped in your own lies. Someone who's cleverer than you will see through the stories.

Another friend of mine, **Lily**, grew up in an emotionally abusive home.

> *My father was very controlling and dominated the family. He would always tell me to talk about how great our family was, how loving it was, even after I left home and went out into the world. I realize now that he was trying to conceal the pain we were all feeling by building a false appearance around our family. We looked like the perfect family on the outside—parents with good jobs, good schools and two cars at home—but inside, it was a different story. Still, when in society, I had to keep up the lies to hide the shame I felt.*

But who do we know who's perfect? Even the greatest athletes, the smartest business people, the high-end socialites are riddled with defects. It is in recognizing our defects that makes us human, and even more so, you can relax when you are yourself.

Imagine going to a social function and not caring how you appear, not worrying about impressing anyone, just jumping into any conversation without giving a thought as to how you will be judged or criticized. Would you look like an ass? Come across as flamboyant or a real jerk? Would you be remembered the next day?

The people who are real are those who attract the most friendships. They are liked not because of whom they know or for what they've achieved, but because they can show others that you don't have to have the best of anything to be good enough.

Good enough is who you are. If you strive for that perfect image, you'll always struggle to be good enough, and you'll never reach your goal of total self-acceptance.

Social Inferiority Relaunch Plan

1. List the traits, skills, and abilities that define you as a unique individual.

We are all unique in the sense that we all have something to offer this world in regard to positive traits. You need to get clear about what your unique traits are so that you can share them without feeling embarrassed or ashamed. I'm always amazed when I ask people what they like about themselves and they say, "Nothing really," or "I'm not good at anything."

We are all good at something, and in most cases, we are great at a couple of things. So what skills do you have? These skills can be social or personal. Maybe you're great at organizing social events.

2. Make a list of your character defects.

Now, how are these defects different from what anyone else experiences? Are your reasons valid? What makes them valid?

You might be ashamed of your defects or flaws. But who doesn't have a flaw? Even the leaders of countries, sports heroes and people of incredible influence have flaws. Maybe we can't always see them, but they're there. Yet, they manage to do their jobs and function at the level they are responsible for. And, so can we.

You have spent many years thinking very negatively about yourself. This has, in a huge way, impacted your self-esteem and social confidence. But the good news is, most of these things are lies. All the bad stuff we have been telling ourselves are just old recordings playing over and over. It's only true if you believe it. And, if it really is true—such as, "I'm a big procrastinator"—well, you can change that.

Procrastination isn't set in stone. You were not born with defects; we create them and give them power. We can turn our defects into positive traits.

3. Identify your internal flaws and escape strategy.

What are the flaws you have that are very difficult to change? If you were to change them, would it make you a better person? Is this a physical or mental flaw? Has it stopped you from moving forward? What is your number one escape strategy? How do you avoid people or social groups? How do you isolate? At what point do you feel the need to run away, and what triggers this action?

Create a list of these flaws. Then, come up with one small action you can take towards changing your flaw. It's important to note that, you should only consider changing this if it is a barrier to your personal growth.

Also, identify the escape strategies you use. Observe how you resist and push away the circumstances that create stress and worry. Then, visualize yourself taking action towards this pain point. Push yourself to chip away at the resistance to move forward.

When you stop running and giving into your avoidance tactics, you are embracing your personal power. This can only elevate your confidence by toughening up your mind to handle situations that you once labeled too difficult to handle.

CHAPTER 7

Trapped by the
Failure Mindset

*"Winners are not afraid of losing. But losers are.
Failure is part of the process of success. People who
avoid failure also avoid success."*

— **Robert T. Kiyosaki**, Author of
Rich Dad, Poor Dad

Failing in life is an inevitable outcome. Try to think back to a time in your life when you succeeded at everything. Chances are, you can't think of a time like that, because all of us have failed at something: You've failed at tests, sports, relationships, and work-related tasks. In every aspect of our lives, making mistakes and what we classify as "failing" should actually be seen as progress.

Some people see failure as something to be feared and avoided. They stay away from pushing beyond their limits because failing is demoralizing, emotionally painful and reduces self-esteem.

There are others who see failing as a necessary step to getting to where they need to go. On the other side of failure is everything you've ever wanted. But if you fear it, you'll spend your life trapped in a bubble and unable to break free.

Which kind of person are you?

Failing can induce stress and makes us question our worth and competency. We experience deep fears driven by anxiety. Failure and the fear it creates are persuasive and manipulative. We become convinced that we have no chance and so we leave all risk on the table and opt for the easy way out. But the easy way is the path to losing everything you could be gaining.

Are you ready to give up, walk away and let failure rob you of all you could have if you were willing to take risks? I didn't think so. That is why this chapter is probably the most critical.

Now, take a minute to consider these questions:

- *Do you minimize your achievements and believe your success isn't justified?*

- *Do you think that you haven't accomplished as much as others, and that you need to prove yourself even further?*

- *Are you attached to the failures of your past, and do you believe they'll be your future?*

- *Are you avoiding any form of responsibility because you want to avoid failing?*

Trapped by Failure

People who struggle with a failure mindset have been subjected to:

- Harsh criticism

- Rejection issues

- Perfectionistic ideals

- Unrealistic expectations

- Humiliating moments

- Lack of belief in themselves and from others

- Lack of love (from childhood and personal relationships)

When we are made to believe we are worthless, it creates deeper feelings of defectiveness. We then carry this feeling of defectiveness into every aspect of our lives. We develop a self-defeating mindset that we are never good enough no matter what we do, and that failing is an expectation we learn to live with.

For example, we choose relationships with people who end up controlling or mistreating us. You might take on a role in your job because it places you in a position of power over others. You don't try anything new because you expect to fail before you even do anything. Just the thought of facing your fear of failure creates anxiety and social exclusion.

The most obvious failures we have all experienced can be observed by everyone: a bad report card in school, losing a client in your business, or a failed relationship, such as a bad breakup or marriage. But the failure nobody can see is the only one you know about: **the failure of self.** It is the most painful failure of all because it is internal.

When we fail, it validates all the reasons we have that we are no good. But here's the truth: Nobody is born a failure. It happens from years of negative conditioning. We are trained to fear failing and therefore, conditioned to fear change. By resisting failing in life, you are choosing to escape. Our avoidance strategies are what keep us stuck in a perpetual loop of self-defeat.

Before we go any further, I want you to make a **failure list**. Write down all the things you feel you have failed at, such as relationships, jobs, or anything in which you think you failed to meet your expectations for yourself or others.

Here is my short list:

1. Failed grade 10 math twice

2. Failed 3x at starting my own business

3. Failed my driving test twice times

4. Failed in many relationships (but learned a lot, too)

5. Failed to graduate from high school with the rest of my class (later, I had to take online classes to pass)

I failed at a lot of things, but I succeeded at many as well. Through making mistakes, I learned about everything that doesn't work. This is how we can close the gap on our errors and move closer to success.

Next, make a list of ten things you have succeeded at that you are happy with. You can follow up on how your failures in life later turned into successes. For example, I failed at business several times. But, I eventually succeeded as well because I stayed with it. I failed courses in school like many people, but it only made me more determined to succeed. Eventually I would go on to college and graduate.

Failure does not have to be a permanent condition, as we will see. You might not succeed today at what you are striving for, but eventually, if you stick and keep working at it with a driven passion, you'll look back someday with gratitude for the lesson the struggle taught you.

If you are ready, let's take a look at the fear of failure, what it does, where it comes from and the strategies we can implement and put into action for recovery.

The Anatomy of a Failure Mindset

My father was a very successful man. He excelled in business and was a leader in his industry for many years. The companies he worked for throughout his 35-year career paid him well, and he was flown all over the country to attend conferences and deliver speeches. But he had one fatal flaw that nobody knew about: He believed he was worthless at his core, a failure, and constantly came up short when he compared himself to his competition.

From the outside, he appeared to be highly successful with a secure job, credentials, a big house, and a yacht. But it wasn't enough. He struggled to accept himself as he was, striving instead to become someone he respected and admired. The battle he fought wasn't with his competitors in business. It was with himself.

One night, he told me this story. "There I was in this boardroom with these other business people. Some of them were billionaires and men with empires. They would look at me and ask me for my opinion on how they should close a deal or beat their competition. Whenever this happened, all I could think about was, 'What are you asking me for? I only have a grade 11 education!'"

My father never finished high school, and he carried it with him throughout his entire life. His parents thought he should quit and get a real job. Because of a lack of support at home with parents who didn't care much for his future, he stopped going to school. But he was a smart man and he wanted to succeed.

He worked hard to get to an executive level in his industry, but the feeling of failure always stuck. He never deemed himself worthy to be in a room with a bunch of other people who had degrees, billions of dollars, and lived in houses larger than most small towns. He spent much of his life trapped in the fear of failing because he listened to his negative voices feeding him false messages that appeared real.

The voices from our past, and the negative actions that were done to us, largely shape the level of success we experience. It is an enigma how someone who achieves more than the average person can still deem themselves unworthy no matter what they've obtained.

You might be successful, but until you accept that you're good enough and that everything you have is a gift that requires gratitude, you will always be poor. I have met many people in life who had it all externally, but internally they were completely bankrupt and could never enjoy what they had.

Not only do we fear failing, but we live it. We walk around with the belief that we're not good enough. We work hard, play hard, and take life very seriously so as not to let our guard down. We have this ongoing feeling of shame, as if we are embarrassed to be ourselves and would rather be someone else.

Just like the social level of self-defeat, we don't deem ourselves worthy of having, being or owning anything. We enter relationships with dependence issues, and we carry around a heavy burden. We feel incomplete.

"If only I can prove myself with one more success, more money, or a higher social status."

This is a perpetual self-defeating cycle that never stops. Not until we put an end to it through creating a stream of thinking that lifts up our negativity.

It has nothing to do with success. You don't get over failure by succeeding and racking up achievements.

If you struggle with the failure mindset, you might have a few or all of these characteristics. This isn't a quiz; use this to identify the core traits you use most often.

You are deeply entrenched in a failure mindset if you:

- Pursue success relentlessly but you're never satisfied.

- Can never measure up to the people you compare yourself to.

- Minimize your skills, abilities, and capacity for success.

- Feel like a phony and believe others will find you out sooner or later.

- Set yourself up for failure because if you succeed, you'll be given more responsibility that you feel sure you'll fail at.

- Believe the worst about yourself, and that every new challenge presented is another chance for you to screw up.

- Obsess about what others think of you, causing you to exaggerate and make things up.

- You do as little as possible to avoid standing out.

- You're afraid of making commitments.

- You have an expectation of failure, so you sabotage your chances of succeeding before you even try.

External Appearance vs. Internal Convictions

If you are trapped in a failure mindset, you are in a lot of internal pain that nobody can see or feel but you. You know it is there because you feel it every day, like a secret you keep close to the surface but just deep enough that it stays hidden.

Nobody knows your fear like you do. So to keep this secret buried, you avoid taking risks. Your failure mindset is what holds you back, and you're paralyzed to move ahead or draw attention to yourself. You're terrified that you might be asked to take on greater responsibility, and risk feeling shame. You'd rather operate from behind the fragile walls of your ego and fear-based mindset.

The Critics and People Who Are Wrong

When it comes to failure, we are our own worst critics. The world around us doesn't have to do anything to contribute to our feelings of inferiority. We can do enough of that ourselves. On the surface, we can appear confident, in control, and be the one making the big decisions.

But the real battle is the internal struggle we cope with day-to-day. It is facing that inner sense of failure. You might appear to have it together, but inwardly, you are terrified of being exposed as the fraud you believe you are.

Struggling to cope with your inner feelings of perfection, shame and failure, your ability to believe in yourself is diminished. You think that no matter what you do, it'll never be good enough.

Perhaps you had a similar experience as a child, causing this belief. The feeling of not being able to measure up, the idea that you might disappoint someone—usually your parents—or your tendency to destroy your chances of success through self-sabotage.

Why would we sabotage ourselves? There are several reasons. First, if you set yourself up to fail, nobody will expect anything from you. You'll be left alone, which is what most people who struggle with their negative emotions long for. We want the world to act as if we don't exist. This way, nobody is watching. You can live your life in peace with your negative vices and nobody will criticize you, either.

By self-sabotaging, the pressure is off and now we can validate all of our excuses for not trying anything. "You see, I told you it was too difficult," or how about, "That's the last time I try that." But sabotage is a method for escape. It is a survival mechanism we have developed to avoid the pain of facing failure.

The self-sabotage strategy is like a silent enemy. We don't know it's there until we look for it. If you have a pattern or history of failing at something, chances are you already know this subconsciously. Now is your chance to bring it to the surface and expose it for what it is. You can only stop destructive behavior when you see the power it has and how it is manipulating your actions.

Here is what **Brian** shares:

> *I was never good in school. At least, that's what I thought. I failed at most courses and rebelled in class when it came to studying. I was often scolded for behavioral problems. I realize I actually wanted help, but I had no help at home and the teachers wanted nothing to do with me because they thought I was just trouble. So I spent lots of time in detention or getting kicked out of class. The more I failed in school, the worse my saboteur patterns became. Self-sabotage is a means of coping with the belief that you're a failure. "If I can't succeed, I'll destroy my chances."*

It is a form of rebellion and a cry for help. But when we can't ask for help, we seek attention. This is brought on by feelings of failure as children.

As children we were often:

- Criticized

- Pushed to succeed and berated when we didn't

- Expected to meet certain criteria before we were given love

- Scrutinized for trying to be different or unique

Escape Methods

First of all, now we know that we use avoidance tactics to sabotage ourselves so we don't have to be responsible for our successes or failures.

But the road seems almost impossible to navigate when there are obstacles at every corner. And if you are like me, you've been maneuvering around difficult obstacles most of your life. It is exhausting. Throughout our lives, escape has become a default action when we wanted to avoid failing. Relationships, work or personal issues are abandoned. Problems are not dealt with but instead pushed aside.

There are several tactics we use to practice avoiding what we don't want to deal with. You might procrastinate and put things off indefinitely or distract yourself with other tasks to avoid the things that demand your attention. Escape is a means of sabotage. You can run, but you'll never recover. We can only get better if we take a stand and choose to not be defeated.

Years ago, when I first noticed my methods of escape, I could see the patterns I was practicing almost on a daily basis. I would avoid talking about difficult subjects such as relationship problems. My attitude was, "It will work itself out." But then it was either handled by someone else, or it was not taken care of at all.

Problem avoidance is an escape from reality. It is a tactic for survival. Because we never learned to deal with our reality as children, we have developed our own methods of coping. It may not be healthy, but it creates a feeling of inner security. We learned to survive because we had no choice.

When the world makes you feel like you are no good, you seek to escape from it.

Procrastination and Minimizing

Similar to problem avoidance, procrastination is a powerful self-defeating habit that can develop from childhood. It holds us back from taking action. It ruins our chances for moving forward.

This is **Ben's** experience:

> *As a kid, I remember hating homework. I would never do my schoolwork. If something were due, I'd wait till the last minute to do it, or maybe not do it at all. I would put everything off. Eventually it became a habit. My father never thought I'd amount to much so I lived up to his expectations. I would sabotage my education just to show him he was right.*

To avoid failing, procrastination is the number one choice for many. It is a form of self-sabotage on many levels. It is a vicious cycle of self-defeat. Of course, many people procrastinate to varying degrees, but some of us have turned it into a habit of survival.

When it is the first default factor that we turn to for escape, it puts everything on hold. You cannot recover when you are busy burying the pain. The opposite of procrastination is taking massive action. These are the action steps that move you out of your pain.

Brushing off praise is another method of avoidance, but with this tactic, you are **minimizing** your achievement because you believe it is worthless. You think anybody could have done it, so it wasn't a big deal. You'll just try harder the next time to do a better job.

By minimizing your own success, you never actually crawl out of the self-pity failure rut. You continue to go for the next big win, but it doesn't last long.

The Failure Mindset Relaunch

Now that we have looked at this mindset in detail, let's get into the strategies we can use to relaunch your action plan. I am going to lay out four strategies you can put into action to recover from and mend your failure mindset.

I suggest you focus on just one strategy at a time. Don't overwhelm yourself and think you have to heal in a week. This long process of relaunching your life cannot be rushed. We are not going for perfection; rather, we are focusing on progress.

1. Talk back to the negative mindset.

There are people in our past who wronged us. They treated us unfairly, criticized our mistakes, and made us feel as if we were major disappointments. When we return to this point in our past, it brings up painful memories. But we need to examine it because we tried to avoid the reality of what happened.

The things we ignore eat away at us over time. This leads to depression, anger, and deep hurts that never have time to heal. We can heal this now.

Confront the people you're angry with. Imagine what it would be like to visit this person and tell them how you feel. What are you going to say? This exercise will free you of your shame. Stay firm and don't think for a minute that you deserved to be punished or treated the way you were. If that person were standing in front of you right now, how would you react? What would you say? What would you hold back on?

The fact is, we can't always confront the people that we're still angry or bitter towards. In many cases, we can't do that anyway, or in cases where abuse happened or there's deep emotional scarring, it might be better to stay your distance. But an exercise that works is to imagine this person is with you and you have five minutes to tell them how you feel. Visualize the conversation and how you are able to express your feelings.

You'll find that you can strengthen your ability to forgive. But this isn't necessarily for the other person to feel better. It is for you. By being able to let go of the pain of what happened, you are freeing yourself up for some serious growth to happen. As long as we stay resentful, angry and bitter, it becomes nearly impossible to move on. You owe it to yourself to level up and step up.

The last chapter in this book is going to walk you through the steps for crafting out a new life for yourself and how to put your dream into practice. We are taking ourselves from the failure mindset model to a completely new way of life. If I am going to fail at something, let it be at what I love to do.

2. Decide to do something you've been putting off.

What is it you have been avoiding? Now is your chance to make it work. Your decision in the moment will shape all of your days to come from now on. What are you deciding to do? Is it a dream that you once abandoned? Or do you want to reach out to someone you haven't spoken to in a long time?

Recognizing what you are running from is the first step to taking action. Your decisions are powerful. The life you are leading right now has been a direct result of the decisions made by you. The direction of a person's life is decided by the choices made in each and every moment.

Indecision creates worry and fear. But decisions made with intention will create the circumstances of your life, today and thirty years from now.

3. Fail forward. Fail often.

When we fail at something, the first instinct is to pull back, reassess, and then maybe try again. But many people don't try again. They reassess and then try something less risky, taking another predictable path that will guarantee success. You will not fail this way, but you won't succeed either.

The only way forward is to embrace the lessons you learned and go with it. In fact, the people who fail the most, get the most. They get ahead, and they get what they have always wanted. The rest are fighting for the same scraps because they have one thing in common: They are afraid to take massive action and fail forward. Your defeat is a stepping stone. You can only step up when you've taken three steps back.

4. Make a checklist of how you're going to succeed.

This is a powerful task. We know all the ways we have failed. Failure has become our master craft. But what if we carved out a checklist of all the ways we can succeed? For example, here is my short checklist of what I am putting into action for better success:

- Wake up early and exercise.

- Read for thirty minutes a day.

- Take walks more frequently.

- Outline the novel I have always wanted to write.

- Enroll in a course.

- Write a letter to someone who once hurt me detailing how I forgive him or her. Sending this letter is optional.

- Add up what I'm grateful for at the end of each day. The goal is to hit 20 per day.

- Focus on one goal I have always wanted to achieve.

- List my achievements in the last ten years, no matter how small.

Now that we have traversed the troubled waters of the mindset of failure, we have covered a lot of ground here. In the first part of the book, we looked at how we justify our feelings of being no good, and the evidence that has mounted against us. We have seen the ways we stay stuck and how building a positive image for ourselves can get us moving in the right direction.

You have examined how you've placed blame and accepted responsibility for your life so that you can change anything. We have worked on creating a positive image for ourselves and how our unrealistic expectations destroy our chances for having a better life.

Now, we will discuss the titan of self-defeat: **Rejection**. This is the last self-defeating mindset.

CHAPTER 8

Rejection Mindset : The Titan of Self-Defeat

"We all learn lessons in life. Some stick, some don't. I have always learned more from rejection and failure than from acceptance and success."

— Henry Rollins

If you had no fear of rejection, what do you think you would do? If you were completely unafraid of criticism, hearing the word no, or being judged for your work, wouldn't you charge forward fearlessly without concern for what the rest of the world thinks?

If rejection is something you struggle with, we know it isn't that easy to turn away from a rejection experience. It sticks with us for a very long time. Rejection can leave scars that last a very long time.

Not everyone interprets rejection the same way. Some people take rejection as a form of defectiveness or a personal attack on their character. Meanwhile, someone else might let rejection roll off and carry on

300 • SCOTT ALLAN

with the next challenge. Is it the rejection that damages our self-esteem, or how we interpret it? By the time you are finished with this chapter, you'll be looking at rejection—what a friend of mine called the titan of self-defeat—in a different way.

Rejection stems from the core belief that we are not worthy. People who struggle with rejection typically have low self-esteem and place little value on themselves. You might feel that you are rejected by your peers, family, or your spouse. Rejection can show up anywhere in your life. But here is the central idea I want to share with you:

Here is an example. John has been dating Mandy for the past three months. Things are going great. Suddenly, she decides one day that the relationship is over. There isn't any explanation or reason. She has found someone else.

Devastated and confused, John goes through a crushing emotional rollercoaster as he tries to figure out what went wrong. His conclusion is that he's just not good enough for Mandy. The problem must be with him.

"Was it something I did? Something I said?"

> *Nobody is rejecting you more than you are rejecting yourself. Rejection always begins with self-rejection and the expectations that you will be turned down even before you take action.*

We have all been there. Relationships ended, employers chose to let us go, or friends stopped calling for no apparent reason. Our first thought is almost always, "What did I do?" We blame ourselves for every rejection that takes place in our lives, and because we don't always have a direct explanation for it, the only logical reason is it must be something we did.

Why? We can trace it back to childhood. Were you ever rejected, abandoned or criticized when things went wrong? If you didn't comply or perform at a certain level, did your parents or peers judge you for not being good enough? It is possible that you're very aware of your rejection issues. If you think you're the only one, let me put your fears to rest: the fear of rejection is a very normal condition.

It is a basic need for everyone to feel loved, accepted, valued, wanted, and appreciated. If we don't get these things, we go through a rejection-depression phase. We feel devalued and unwanted. This turns to shame and the belief that we are not good enough for their world. Uncertainty sinks in. You question your self-worth. You might go to extremes to gain acceptance, such as people pleasing or doing things for people that would ordinarily go beyond your level of acceptance.

If you grew up in an environment in which stability was an issue and love was withheld, the condition of rejection is one of your self-defeating traits. It is the titan of self-defeat for a reason. It's very hard to recover from this condition. Not impossible, just very difficult.

That is why we're looking at it last as the core negative condition.

Rejection Expectation

Our flaws are so painfully obvious to us that we expect to be rejected in just about every situation. Rejection expectation is the condition of rejecting yourself before the other person has a chance. You think so little of yourself that you are convinced you will be ignored or mistreated.

Picture yourself in a social situation, such as a party. The person you're with suddenly has to leave, and you view this interaction as a rejection. We are so tuned in to our rejectionist selves that we start to see it everywhere.

In most cases, the other side has no idea what is going on. Most people aren't thinking, "I'm going to reject this person by turning my back on him." Chances are, the other person has an agenda we know nothing about. And it has nothing to do with us.

This internal fear is what's holding you back. On top of that, you have the core belief that you are no good and that you are so unimportant that people will lose interest in you within a matter of minutes.

When it comes to socializing with new people, I am terrible at it. My rejection radar is so tuned up that I am just waiting for someone to figure out that I'm not good enough to be here. When I shared this with a friend of mine who is a social relationship expert, he said, "Are you sure? You really think anyone at the party showed up with an agenda to reject you? People are too preoccupied with themselves. Get over it."

Great advice. He took a complicated issue I had been struggling with and narrowed it down to the essentials: "Nobody cares. They are too worried about themselves."

It sounds like such a simple concept, but let's think about it. Does anyone really wake up and decide that today is the day they're going to target someone and reject them? No, and the truth is, we all reject something or someone in our day-to-day interactions. We are just not aware of it.

Self-Rejection

What if I told you that 90 percent of the time, it was you rejecting yourself instead of the world rejecting you? Would you believe me? Probably not. You would start to validate the reasons why you are rejected and make it into a real condition with all the evidence you've collected. Failures at school, relationships, or people who always say no when they should be saying yes.

When someone says no, it means there's another opportunity out there. You are turned down for a job, and then a week later you get a better one. You get turned down for a bank loan, and a week later the market collapses. Someone breaks up with you, and you meet someone who's 10 times better for you. Who really knows if rejection is good or bad?

I don't think rejection is either good or bad. It is just a part of our lives. It's an understanding of perspective, and when you can accept yourself just as you are without worrying what others are thinking, you'll appear less fearful with less anxiety. But if you try to avoid it through escape or distraction by purposefully navigating away from it, you are giving up the opportunity for something better.

Rejection isn't always personal.

Let's be honest. Rejection is, at times, personal. Somebody doesn't like you for whatever reason. It has happened to me throughout my life and it continues to happen. But there are lots of people who do like me. Some reject my opinion and even my offer to help, but they'll take it from someone else. Rejection is a numbers game. Some will and some won't. When we make it personal, we are putting our feelings out there and letting them take a beating.

Rejection is an opinion.

It is based on the other person's ideals. And, in most cases, it is more about whether or not you have what they want at that time. For example, I was rejected many times for employment, based not on my character but on my skill set. This had nothing to do with me as an individual. They were looking for a particular type of skill regardless of the person behind the skill.

The fear of judgment.

This is where people realize the one thing they have been avoiding: the fear of being judged. Rejection, inferiority, and the fear of criticism all boils down to judgment.

I want you to think back to a point in your childhood when someone, most likely a parent, judged or criticized you for being you. Think about that moment. Was it a bad report card? Failing to make the team? Or maybe you were just clumsy in social situations and brought embarrassment to the family.

Whatever it may be, rejection has its origins in the judgment and condemnation you perceived growing up. Now, in adulthood, you still feel that pain. When you have moments of doubt and you are wondering if you are ever good enough, you are tapping in to that pain you had growing up. It sticks like butter and it doesn't leave until you wipe it off.

People form opinions about others all the time. When was the last time you assumed something about someone before having all the evidence? Chances are, you were convinced it was the right opinion and that your judgment was sound. You were sure nothing would change your mind.

Now, how many times do others form opinions about you? You probably don't know, because we're being scrutinized and judged all the time. We just don't know it. We either pretend it isn't happening or we minimize it by attacking others before we can be attacked.

But wouldn't it be a good assumption to know that most people are probably wrong about their opinions. We think we are right, but how do we know? We believe we have the right to reject, judge and condemn, so we do it.

But while it happens to us, we retaliate by dishing out our own pain. It makes the world an easier place to live in if we can put up our barriers and get ready to defend ourselves.

Desensitize Yourself.

One of the strategies I teach to overcome rejection is to desensitize yourself to it. How is this done? Desensitization is like emotional conditioning for the mind. The more you are rejected, the less it hurts. But what we fear in this case is the initial pain of going through that rejection. It is the first sting that hurts the most, and it's the one pain point we try to avoid.

When we stop taking risks, such as approaching people for conversation or asking someone out on a date, we might be saving ourselves from the pain of getting turned down. But there is another side to this we need to seriously consider. You are also missing out on something much bigger than an emotional hurt.

Think about this. You meet someone you like and you want to ask that person out for dinner. But you don't. You've been burned before. Someone has broken up with you and this reinforced your beliefs that you are unlovable, unwanted, and unworthy. This fear is deeply ingrained. You've been alone for years because of it, and now, years later that barrier still stands between you and what you really want.

You decide to do nothing. And in making that decision, you get nothing. Yet, you save yourself from the pain of being rejected.

But what about the other side of the story? Sweating with fear and your heart pounding, you take a chance, ask that person out, and they say yes. You end up spending a lifetime with this person, and you know that the only reason is because you took a chance to face your moment of fear.

Go out there and create more of these opportunities to get rejected. Make it a numbers challenge. See how many people say yes when you ask them to have coffee with you. How many agree to have their picture taken with you? Try approaching strangers and having an open conversation. You'll be amazed to find out that you're not the only one with fear. We all have it.

Detach yourself from expectations and focus on the action of approach. Even if you're told no, it's still a win because you've approached someone and asked them for something.

The Lies We Believe

When we avoid going after the things we truly want, we are denying ourselves so much more. For what? The pain of hearing no, or being humiliated, or experiencing vulnerability. Mind you, these are real emotions and we can't ignore them. But allow them to govern our actions and they will create your destiny of living in fear.

We take rejection personally. After all, it's an attack on character and ego. When someone tells you they don't want you and don't need you, it is very painful. Can you imagine being told this as a child, or being treated that way by a parent?

Rejected children are hit the hardest, and I have met many people to this day who struggle with it. But I have also met many who faced this struggle and managed to persevere. If they hadn't overcome what was keeping them trapped, they would have been trapped forever.

Take a moment to think about all the ways you avoid being rejected. Make a list of them right now.

Here is the list I came up with.

- Avoiding eye contact

- Saying no to social events

- Choosing to be alone rather than with others

- Not applying for the job that I really want

- Staying away from training events

- "Forgetting" to show up for an exam

- Ignoring the sudden conversation strangers try to engage you in

- Not writing that book

- Avoiding asking for a discount

- Avoiding joining sports teams

We escape the risk of rejection through avoidance. We stay away from the fear of failing or looking stupid, and we miss out on so much more.

We deal with and get over rejection by pushing ourselves out there, taking that risk, and trying something even if we're afraid we'll fail. By taking a risk at failing, you are gaining an important lesson—learning to accept that not everything in life is a *yes*.

Driven by feelings of low-esteem and low self-worth, we do not deem ourselves important or deserving enough. And because we take rejection personally, it feels like a physical and emotional attack on our confidence when we are abandoned or turned away.

The experience places you back in that moment in time when you first became aware of the feeling of rejection—a parent critiqued you, perhaps you had a sibling who always seemed better than you, or the neighborhood kids singled you out for being different. Rejection is experienced and you live that pain again and again. It becomes a part of you, until you have built up a thick emotional shield that keeps the world out and locks you inside.

And this is when the real hurt begins. In protecting ourselves from rejection, we lock ourselves on the inside and throw away the key. Nobody can get in and you can't break out. I don't know about you, but that doesn't seem like living to me.

The more we stay hidden, the more severe the feelings of loneliness. Then, over time, as we watch other people get on with their lives, we recognize the life of isolation we opted in for. By staying scared and protecting ourselves from taking any form of risk, we ended up with far less than we deserved.

And, we deserve a whole lot more.

The Rejection Free Action Plan

These are the steps I use in my rejection free seminars and action plans for breaking free of rejection. There isn't any magic formula. These steps are as much common sense as walking to get from A to B. But when it comes to rejection, there is very little that has to do with common sense. We are dealing with a condition that has had control over you for as long as you can remember.

People handle it differently as well. For example, we have no problem functioning in a workplace. We can take risks, make decisions, and everything is normal. But in a relationship, things fall apart for you. You become needy and anxious over getting rejected by the person you're involved with. The pain point you had when you were growing up is likely the one that will be activated.

1. The rejection isn't real.

I know this may sound crazy but think about it for a minute. You show up for a job interview, it goes really well, and then they call you several days later to tell you that weren't selected. Why? You didn't have the proper skills for the job.

You now have two choices: 1. You can accept what they have said to you as positive feedback. 2. You can go out and get trained for that skill set you are lacking.

This is you taking positive action. The other option is, you can throw away your résumé and give up, going back to the job you hate because that's the only thing you're good at.

2. The rejection you experience is as real as you make it.

We have a choice about whether or not to give rejection power over us. Or, we can seize that power for ourselves and do something positive with it. Ten people say no to you? Somebody is bound to say yes. Ten people break up with you? That eleventh person recognizes the best parts in you and sticks around.

Here are a few examples:

- You're not her type. Then go find someone who enjoys your company.

- You ask for a discount and the salesman says no. Okay, they don't discount those products. Let it go.

- Your book gets rejected because the publisher says it's the worst thing he has ever read. But don't forget someone once said the same thing to Stephen King.

- You go to a party and get ignored by most of the guests. Perhaps they're snobs and you're not their type anyway. Go someplace else.

It is perspective on a gigantic scale and you can be in charge of the outcome instead of letting the results fail you when it doesn't work out the way you expect.

3. Detach yourself from the outcome.

Typically speaking, detaching from things is a major challenge for most people. If you could just "let it go and let God," as they say in AA, would you be so hung up on rejection in the first place? No. You'd be able to take each rejection easily. But we are sensitive people and when criticized, ignored, or worried about what others think of us, we cling to the opinions of others as if they meant everything.

4. Stay centered in your own emotional playground.

What happens when your emotions are governed by the emotions of other people? When they are angry, you feel tense and nervous. If they are happy or in a good mood, you feel relaxed and at ease. By seeking that approval that rarely comes in our relationships at home or at work, we are forever being pulled back and forth.

A strong mentor of mine once shared a piece of solid advice. He said, "When others are in control of how you react, they've got you. I mean, how can you be happy or feel anything that is real when the weight of your emotional state is dependent on somebody else? When we fear someone is going to disapprove of us, we keep trying to gain his or her acceptance. Even if you get it, you haven't really gained anything until you've accepted yourself."

Your emotional playground is the area you control. Others can come in to play, but at the end of the day, this area belongs to you. By staying centered in our own emotional backyard, you can own the feelings that you frequently lose touch with. For example, some kids come into your playground and they are in a bad mood. They try to disrupt things by taking control, scaring the other kids, or being hard to get along with.

Give them what they want and they persist with the behavior. Instead, draw the line on your boundaries, and let them know they can stay as long as they behave. This is how we can monitor and maintain our emotions in almost any situation. When we fear rejection, hide our shame or try to escape, we are not centered in our own backyards. We are playing in someone else's.

It takes practice and concentration to stay aware of how you are feeling. When you feel it coming on, that's a warning sign that your fear is being triggered. You can stop this from spiraling out of control. First, say no to the loss of control. You have nothing to lose.

I have a tactic set up for this. When I am in a situation in which I feel afraid, such as when I have to speak publicly, I say to myself, "No, I'm not letting this happen." I give myself permission to have full control over what I feel and how I perform. Reacting to fears and running just keeps the cycle going.

5. Give up the need for approval.

You don't need permission to feel good about yourself. The experience you've had in regard to your need for approval, struggling with self-esteem and fighting off defectiveness is, "I'm no good unless somebody tells me I am." It just isn't true, but you have to work on communicating with your child from the past. Painful as it may be at times, it is also very liberating and when you practice this consistently, it becomes a habit that heals and transforms your pain.

6. Focus on what you can control.

When we react to the actions and attitudes of others, it has a negative effect on us. If you take responsibility for this, it feeds in to your rejectionist persona. You can control how you think. You can create your own thoughts at will. This can generate the emotion you want to feel.

When we are feeling rejected, in most cases it is us rejecting ourselves. We can put an end to this by putting confidence into our body movements. In chapter 11 we will discuss in more detail the power of body control and how using eye contact and posture triggers your feelings and thoughts to follow the body movement.

When others treat us badly or you are trying too hard to please someone else, you become reactive to their moods. They are controlling you. This leads to a rejection set up. You are eventually going to get hit hard when they decide they want to take an emotion out on you.

Take notice when you are switched to reactive mode. You will know because you'll feel as if you're waiting for the hammer blow to fall. It creates anxiety and switches on your escape trigger.

Monitor your thoughts. When negative thinking skips in and starts to carry you on that downward spiral, you can stop and say, "No. This isn't happening now. I won't allow it." I use this tactic several times a day. It works because it acts as a trigger disruptor

You can put an end to this type of negative behavior but only when you're tuned in to what is happening within you. Don't let others get into your head. Stay centered. Remind yourself how far you've come and that every day is the day you are relaunching your life for a better one. Nobody is going to reject you unless you give them permission to do so. You decide what you're worthy of having, doing, and being.

Section III:
Relaunch Your Life

"Recognizing that you are not where you want to be is a starting point to begin changing your life.

— **Deborah Day**

CHAPTER 9

Creating a Positive
Self-Image

*"Your attitude is like a box of crayons that color
your world. Constantly color your picture gray, and
your picture will always be bleak. Try adding some
bright colors to the picture by including humor, and
your picture begins to lighten up."*

— Allen Klien

Wouldn't it be nice if we were handed a blueprint from birth, a roadmap for creating a life of love, acceptance, and well-being? A blueprint that outlined the best principles of life for creating an absolutely perfect positive you? I don't know about you, but I'd be very interested in getting my hands on such a thing.

However, life doesn't work that way. For most people, a positive self-image is something that takes a lot of effort. The world is a volatile place and our positive self-image is constantly under attack. It feels as if we're defending our territory against all the negative influencers out there.

This is part of the great challenge. In this book, we have discussed the negative emotions that attack our positive selves. Despite our best intentions, we feel ourselves being pulled back by these forces that continue to chip away at us.

The "Positive You" Blueprint

First of all, let me ask you these questions. Take your time to think about them if needed. Your answers will help to clarify the best path to take when it comes to building and creating your positive self-image.

Questions for thought:

1. *What are you feeling about yourself right now?*

2. *If someone asked you, "Are you successful?" what would you say?*

3. *If someone asked you, "Are you a failure?" what would you say?*

4. *If someone asked you to define yourself in twenty words or less, how would you respond?*

5. *After reading through the four negative mindsets, what mindset impacts you the most? How has this affected your positive self-image?*

6. *Who are you blaming for the negative experiences in your life? Are you ready to let this go?*

How to Protect Yourself Against Image Destroyers

Creating a positive image of the person you want to be is highly recommended. But how do you protect yourself against the people who criticize, attack or try to undermine you in some way? These types of people are detrimental to our mental health.

First of all, if you struggle with self-esteem issues, or are overly sensitive to criticism and rejection, being around people who are looking for someone to target is going to create a stressful situation. If you were raised by a critical parent or you endured years of rejection, you are most likely sensitive around people whom you know are 'image destroyers.' They basically seek out prey and look for areas of weakness to attack.

We could experience this in love relationships, marriage, or through coworkers. If you find yourself in the company of an image destroyer, how do you deal with that? If you are working on your positive image, being surrounded by this tension is going to rip at your mental health.

Here are the strategies for bringing more self-love and acceptance into your life.

1. Identify the image destroyer.

The first step is to identify the person and tag them as an image destroyer. These people may appear overly aggressive, or they might have passive aggressive tendencies. They are nice to you one minute but they'll turn on you the next. When we encounter these people, we are tempted to walk on eggshells around them. It's like trying to maneuver around a sleeping giant. You don't want to cause trouble so you play it safe, hoping that they don't find out how sensitive you are.

The bottom line here is to stand up for yourself. When you encounter people who are critical, angry, or demanding, it has nothing to do with you. It is about perception. They are as strong as we make them out to be.

2. **Realize that it isn't all you.**

I have encountered several people who were image destroyers. They looked for the opportunity to attack, criticize or shame someone. It isn't pretty, but they exist, and we need to protect ourselves so they don't damage our positive self-image. It is important to remember that we are not the problem.

Most people you will work with or interact with may be fair, respectful, and professional. But image destroyers are different. They tend to make their own rules and expect you to follow them. It could be a manager, a neighbor, or depending on the nature of your relationships, someone in your immediate family.

Here, **Karen** tells us her story:

> I was married for several years and things were great. Then one day it just changed. My husband became emotionally abusive and over time it escalated to the point I was nearly crazy. I thought it was all me and that if I changed, things would go back to normal, the way it was. But the more I tried,

the worse it got. He would look for any chance to put me down or belittle me, often in front of friends or at a party. Until I had broken away, my self-image was completely destroyed.

One core reason we struggle with self-image is because we are dealing with so many conflicting negative emotions. We want to be more positive but are plagued by negative thoughts. We want to be more assertive and proactive but we deal with self-criticism. We desire to connect and interact at a deeper level with others, but find ourselves isolating instead.

Take a minute to think about the image you have of yourself. When you really connect with your personality and character, how do you feel about who you are? Do you feel weak or strong? Do you have a negative or a positive image of yourself?

When we look back at all of the negativity we have survived over the years, is it really that surprising that the image and vision we have of ourselves is weak? Identifying where you are with your self-image is the first step to massive change. You have to see yourself as you are, and then you need to visualize yourself as you want to be.

Many people are stuck because they are sitting at phase one, and they only see themselves as who they are. To make it worse, they are hooked in to listening to the old recordings of the past, feeding negative images into their subconscious all day.

324 • SCOTT ALLAN

Think about this: How would you feel if you listened to a voice inside your mind (not your own) that was feeding you a message that sounded like this:

> *You are nothing. You've always been nothing. Everybody is better than you and, no matter what you do, you'll fail at it. You're ugly and you have no real potential for anything. Just give up before you make a fool out of yourself.*

You might think this is an over-exaggerated example, but many people, even when they're unaware of it, are tapped in to a mental voice that is controlling the show. Most days we don't even know it is there because it's so subtle, like a lion that hides in waiting in tall grass. It's the wounded child who never got to play with the other kids. The one who was criticized, humiliated, abandoned, and learned to fear the world.

You've been kept back from pursuing the life you dreamed of and building the reality that you wanted because somebody else decided long ago that you aren't worthy of having it. It is the voice of reason and damnation that has been controlling your decisions, making choices, and dominating your behavior.

One person said they called it, "The beast that never sleeps." It is more than just a negative voice in your head. Many have bought in to the lie that this is who they are—worthless, useless, or just a plain failure.

Earlier I told you about my father, a successful businessperson, who never believed that he was good enough to be with the "real people." These thoughts and vices, these beliefs, were fed to him throughout years of conditioning.

When you're treated like you're nothing, told lies about what you are worth by the people you trusted the most, it becomes your identity. You absorb this as the only reality you know, regardless of whether it is true or not.

But we know they were wrong. All of them. Your level of success and how you feel about yourself has nothing to do with what anyone else says or does. People with high levels of self-esteem and confidence will tell you: "Bad words roll off me like water off a duck's back." That is fine and we can accept that now, but how about a child who doesn't know any better?

As children, we're forming our own self-images of who we are supposed to be. At that time in our lives, we don't have the experience or maturity to forge our own destiny. So, we do the only thing we know how: We trust the people who are taking care of us to fill in the gaps, teach us about life, and praise our victories whether we win or lose. But it doesn't always happen this way.

Why am I telling you this? So we can learn to understand and accept that whatever happened in the past, while it can't be undone, we can decide now to improve our lives for the future. Nothing happens until you can take a stand and move forward.

It is this attachment to our past pain that is keeping us there. As someone once said to me: "You can always remember the bad stuff that was done, but there is good stuff, too. Take that and move forward with it. When you stick with the 'wounded animal' imposter, it becomes you. Your pain shapes your future."

This brings us to the crossroads. Your self-image is in need of a makeover, and we can start to work on it right here and now. You can decide whether you want to listen to those negative voices or turn them off. You can silence the power they have over you. It begins with a decision.

The "Not Now" Technique

One technique I employed over the years is what I call the "not now" technique. Whenever my mind began racing with fearful, negative thoughts that switched on those voices feeding into my head, I would simply say, "not now" and turn it off.

By inserting these words, I was interrupting the flow of negativity. In doing this, I made myself aware of what was happening instead of just letting it happen. I was free to choose the thoughts I wanted, and create the language that communicates with my mind.

The Five-Minute Mirror Technique

Before I continue, I want you to take some time out. This is a short exercise that is going to be uncomfortable. But to reach where you want to be, you have to get ready for discomfort. The reason you won't like it is because you've possibly been avoiding it.

This mirror technique was taught to me years ago. For five minutes, you are going to have a conversation with your "mirror" self. In this conversation, you will talk about:

- *What you're grateful for in life. Who are you grateful for? Do you have a job you love? Do you live in a nice house?*

- *The traits you like about yourself. Start with one trait. What is it? Are you honest? Do you have integrity? What are you good at?*

- *What are you avoiding? Why? What fears do you have about yourself? About other people?*

Discuss this now with your mirror image. Why a mirror? Well, few of us feel comfortable looking in the mirror and talking to ourselves.

For example: Here's what I didn't like about myself: I would escape from reality. I avoided the things I didn't want to own up to. This habit was very difficult for me to change. But I could change it by recognizing it.

Give yourself five minutes for this. You can even record it and play it back later. This is the real work that makes change possible. But remember, it took years for you to condition yourself to feel bad about who you are. You've worked hard at building negative self-image. Give your mind and heart time to heal. It needs a chance to correct what has been done.

The Formula for Empowering Your Image

It takes time to build up an empowering and confident image of yourself. As we set out to make changes in our emotional and mental states, we find that we are up against those inner voices that won't leave us alone. They are not real. They are simply impressions of old voices and opinions that your mind has recorded. But that doesn't mean they hurt any less. We can control these voices so that they stay silent. After all, you are in total control of your own mind.

Up until now it just appeared that you had no choice in how you were living. But we know that isn't true. You can empower your character to no limits.

How to Overcome Negative Conditioning

It is easy for us to judge others because they can't fight back. But do you consider how the world sees you? Take this a step further. How do you visualize yourself? Are you a positive influence?

For many years, I wasn't. I had a bad habit of seeing the worst in others and using that as a benchmark to sum up their character. But seeing the damaging effect that it had on my emotional well-being, I made a concrete decision not to be that type of person.

We should set boundaries within ourselves. For example, can you catch yourself when you start to criticize your mistakes or when you fail to meet your goals or personal expectations? Do you have healthy boundaries that kick in when you have gone too far in undermining yourself and comparing yourself to other people?

It is one thing when boundaries are elicited upon us. We are expected to follow rules, and many of us do, but how about the rules we set for ourselves?

Draw the line on your negative patterns of defeat. By drawing on your self-actualization, you can consciously choose what is acceptable. You don't have to wait for permission.

CHAPTER 10

The Self-Love Model and Breaking the Negative Cycle

"We are constituted so that simple acts of kindness, such as giving to charity or expressing gratitude, have a positive effect on our long-term moods. The key to the happy life, it seems, is the good life: a life with sustained relationships, challenging work, and connections to community."

— Paul Bloom

This book has a singular focus: to provide you with a better path toward self-love. Yes, loving yourself. The journey toward self-love is a balance of doing things for yourself, and what is expected of you. But what matters isn't what the world expects but what you expect from yourself.

Only you can make yourself happy. I know this sound like arbitrary common sense or old-style advice, but have you ever placed your dependence for love on someone else and ended up disappointed? Exactly. Nobody can provide you 24/7 with that feeling of self-compassion. Nobody can feed you the thoughts that go into creating your positive mindset.

You are the master gardener of your mind, body, and spirit. So, live that way. Do nice things for yourself. Treat your life as if it is a great creation. Do this and you'll always be working on the self-love model.

Throughout this book we looked at the negative mindsets that destroy self-esteem, damage confidence and keep us trapped in our own hell. But these are not who we are. They are obstacles preventing us from becoming what we have always wanted to be. Remove the patterns of defeat and you rise up to be unbeatable.

The Self-Love Model

When you hear the words self-love, what do you think about? I used to hate these words because I didn't love myself very much, and I certainly wasn't going to tell people about it if I did. But what is it, really?

Well, we know what it means to not love ourselves. You may have had deep resentments toward those who harmed you. You probably had many things about yourself you didn't like. Maybe you hated yourself so much you were near self-loathing. Self-loathing is powerful, but so is love. In fact, it's much stronger. Yet, we are conditioned to believe in fear from a very young age.

Self-love is everywhere, but we have kept it hidden all these years. Why? Vulnerability. Shame. Fear. We hide ourselves to protect ourselves. But in protecting who we are, we fail to express who we are. It's a powerful catch-22.

Before you can truly have any balance in your life, and build healthy relationships with the people around you, you need to first develop your relationship with yourself.

But what does it mean to love yourself?

Many people never do. They are taught that success is about getting high grades, achievement, getting a job to justify our purpose, and then finding that special someone who is going to complete us. I have done all these things and I can tell you with confidence, while it helped to contribute to my self-esteem and success, there wasn't much focus on self-actualization. When it came to my achievements, they didn't make me happy for long. Soon I was looking for something else.

Relationships provided me with some sense of what love was supposed to be like, but they eventually failed when they couldn't live up to my needy expectations. I had success in business one day, but a bad day the next. What was missing was a sustainable system that wasn't dependent on some level of success that had to be achieved first.

When I was rejected or told, "Sorry, it just isn't working out," I was convinced that I was unlovable. It turns out that external validation isn't a formula for happiness.

Unconditional Love

I have met many people over the years who confessed that they couldn't feel any sense of love for themselves. When I asked why, they would say, "Nobody ever made me feel lovable." Unconditional love is what we learn from our parents. We either get it or we don't, and if we don't get it, the love we grow up with becomes largely conditional.

We go through life believing that we can be loved once we have achieved a certain level of status. If you were raised in an environment that favors your achievements, you may have received this validation for doing well in school or sports.

"If I get the highest grades in class, my parents will be happy."

"If I do as my wife says, she'll show her appreciation for me."

"If I can live up to the expectations of my boss, she'll respect me."

When we lack that connection to unconditional love, we spend our lives in pursuit of it. It is the quest for validation that we are lovable. But when it comes to unconditional love, aside from our parents, the greatest source comes from within you. Yes, what you are looking for is what you already have. Hollywood has it all wrong.

We are made to think that once we find that special someone, we'll discover that source of power that can provide us with the love we need. But it isn't so. People are people, and what you mistake for unconditional love in the beginning is really the start of a relationship that has yet to discover the flaws of each individual. Many relationships fail because, as they move forward, these flaws become more evident and the illusion is shattered.

We have to **stay grounded** in reality.

Doesn't it feel at times that we are always trying to please, validate, or fulfill someone else's expectations based on performance or achievement? There are some societies that are driven this way. Many individuals as well.

Here is what happens in this case: We move through life focused on doing and not being. Instead of being a person who is worthy of love, you put all your efforts into getting recognition for achievements. But these achievements are short-lived.

As soon as you are done with one achievement, you're on to the next one. It becomes a never-ending cycle without any sustainable results. You're only as good as your last achievement.

Most people lose the concept of unconditional love because they believe love is based on a results-driven achievement.

Here's what **Marty** said about his childhood:

> *I'd be expected to perform well in school. When I did well, my parents bought me a computer. If I did exceptionally well, it was a reward of some sort. But*

once, I got sick and couldn't go to school. My grades and performance went down, and when that happened, I didn't get any rewards. I realized years later that the love I was getting only stuck around as long as I was doing something. It was based on doing and not being.

Imagine two doors:

Door #1: Conditional love is the love we get when we please others. In fulfilling their expectations, we feel like we are doing what is expected of us. Love is justified.

Door #2: Unconditional love is the love we receive when we are just being ourselves. No validation or justification is needed.

I'll take door number two.

Conditional love is based on doing. You have to show that you are worthy before someone will give you the recognition you want. But unconditional love is being, and this is what you can give yourself. The single mistake people make is expecting to draw this from the world.

We have spent a large part of our lives dependent on other people for our needs, and this is especially true when it comes to attracting love. Of course, we can get love from our friends and family. But the real respect is self-respect, self-reliance, and self-trust.

One of the best things you can do for yourself is to live with self-compassion. You've heard of showing compassion to others in hopes that you receive some in return? Well, try turning that around and showing compassion to yourself. After everything you've been through so far, don't you think you deserve it?

You don't have to earn compassion. It is yours. Decide to treat yourself with respect. Make it a daily reprieve. You don't need permission from anyone, and if someone in your life is a compassion thief and holding you back from experiencing your full potential, then it is time to take a look at that relationship.

I have a motto that works for me: Anything or anyone who is a consistent negative force in my life is either helping me to grow as an individual or isn't. If it isn't contributing to your life, it gets the boot. We can only feel good about ourselves when we learn to treat ourselves like valuable human beings.

Open Honesty

You should be honest with yourself as much as possible. Stay true to what you know is right. Accept it when you are feeling fearful and uncertain. This is a sign that you could be slipping back into an old routine. Accept yourself with all your flaws and don't criticize yourself or others for theirs. People will make mistakes and screw things up. That's what we do.

Work your empathy and have an open mind toward people who are trying their best. But be aware of the people you meet who need to be kept at a distance. If they are dragging you down with their issues and problems, but they seem unwilling to do anything about it, cut the ties, and step away from them. To be true to yourself is also about being aware of the people you can't help right now. They are not ready.

Expressing Self-Compassion

As I mentioned earlier, compassion is a positive driving force that we need. Without compassion in your life, specifically directed toward yourself, it's as if you're trying to sail a boat with a hole in it.

Compassion is a weapon against tyranny, animosity, and selfishness. When we create compassion and tap in to the love we can find there, it shifts your mindset from fear-based to empowerment. Self-compassion is the ability to love yourself, not in a narcissistic way, but out of genuine concern for self.

An example would be a person who spent a lifetime stuck in destructive addictions. Bill was trapped in feeling sorry for himself, mired in self-pity, and felt that he had little to contribute to society or humanity.

But Bill also had a strong will to change. When he finally decided to turn it around, he quit most of his addictions and developed his compassion through helping others recover, as well. You can find your compassion by sharing your story with others. There isn't any better way to contributing than helping another person overcome obstacles.

Self-Acceptance

It is hard for many of us to like ourselves as we are. As we truly are, right now, without having an attachment to the past or the future. This is the area in which we fight to balance our lives.

Let's take the past as an example. We have all been through experiences and made mistakes. We have hurt others and we have been hurt. Many hold on to regret and pain from childhood that has morphed over time into a deeper form of negativity that transforms into depression, anger, or rage. The bottom line is, our past selves cannot be corrected, only accepted.

Breaking the Cycle Action Plan

1. 20-minute thought meditation

I love meditation. I didn't do it for the longest time because I couldn't stand to be alone with my thoughts for more than a few minutes. But as I worked through this program, I learned to calm myself down. Now I can meditate for 15 to 20 minutes a day. This has proven to be a very powerful calming exercise. You probably have some idea how it works so I'll just run through the meditation exercise steps again.

1. Play a piece of relaxing music.

2. You can sit in a chair or in a relaxed position.

3. Breathe in and out deeply. Breathe in deeply, and exhale for five seconds.

4. Focus on your thoughts and try to keep them still. You could also run positive affirmations through your mind.

5. Make this a consistent habit you can tap into on a regular basis.

2. Visit your "past" child

Imagine that you could go back in time to visit yourself when you were a kid. Choose a painful memory that you are holding onto. Approach the child version of yourself and embrace him or her. Hold them for as long as you can. Tell them you love them.

If you think this exercise sounds silly and your response is, "No way am I doing that," that's okay, but try it just once. It really is an amazing exercise that works if you keep doing it. You will connect with the biggest part of who you were.

3. Taking care of your health

It amazes me how I see people damaging themselves physically. Eating poorly, smoking, drinking in excess, or overworking. We put ourselves through a lot of pain that isn't reflective of someone who loves themselves. This is the pain point of addictions or activities that damage us.

When we fail to take care of our bodies, we are essentially limiting the long life we could have. Don't you want to live as long as you can? If you were on your deathbed now, wouldn't you long for more time with your children or loved ones? Think about that. If this was your last day on earth, how would you spend it?

Don't end it with regret. If you have some habits that need to be controlled and changed in order to live a healthier lifestyle, then become aware of what they are. Create a vision of yourself who's feeling good because you are looking after yourself.

Change the way you eat. Stop eating anything that is shaving years off your life. Get rid of addictions such as drugs or smoking, all of which robs you of a potentially longer life.

How you treat your body in terms of exercise, eating habits, and addictions is a direct reflection of how you are valuing the life you have. If you don't value your life, you don't love yourself enough. If you are eating badly and taking substances that have long-term damaging effects, you won't enjoy quality of life.

CHAPTER 11

The Power of Confident Body Language

"Don't wait until everything is just right. It will never be perfect. There will always be challenges, obstacles and less than perfect conditions. So what. Get started now. With each step you take, you will grow stronger and stronger, more and more skilled, more and more self-confident and more and more successful."

— Mark Victor Hansen

You are going to start working on your self-image right now, starting today. You don't have to get into any lengthy cognitive exercises or spend years psychoanalyzing yourself. Change begins with simple actions performed consistently over a period of time and with deliberate intent.

We can make ourselves look better, feel better, and drive our confidence to a new level just through implementing confident body language. When we think of healing from our self-defeating patterns we associate it with emotions and mental functions. While this is true, your positive appearance will make you feel great.

Although this book largely focuses on your mindset, being aware of your body language can change everything for you.

There are hundreds of little things that portray how we are feeling inside. With the material you've already learned in this book on creating powerful mindsets for overcoming self-defeat, this chapter on controlling your body language to build confidence will add to your powerhouse of personal development, change and healing.

Here is why. For years, I avoided eye contact with people. It didn't matter if I was ordering coffee at a café or in the middle of a business meeting. I hated eye contact. As someone who has struggled with confidence, self-esteem, and rejection issues, making eye contact was the last thing I wanted to do. It was the most uncomfortable feeling. I remember thinking:

What if they see through me?

What if the look in my eye makes them think I'm lying?

When you struggle with low self-esteem or feelings of vulnerability, it shows up through your body language. For example, you might slouch when you sit or you keep your gaze averted from others. When you walk, you hold your head down with your focus to the ground. In communicating with people, you stand with your arms folded as if defending yourself.

Just take a look around you at the people you see every day. How are they walking? What does their posture, measure of eye contact, and the movement of their hands and feet tell you about them? You can tell a lot about a person's confidence levels just by observing how they move.

Strategies for Positive Eye Contact

The day I became aware of my poor eye contact skills, I had nearly walked into a friend of mine on the street because I hadn't even noticed them. My gaze was downcast as I walked. According to my friend, it was a habit I always had. When I walked, I kept my head down. I wasn't good at making eye contact with people and became aware of my fear if it felt too uncomfortable.

When your focus is on the ground, your head follows and you hang your head low when you walk. Forget about how it makes you look. What matters is how it makes you feel. When I put my head down and walked with my eyes to the ground, I felt weak, vulnerable, and shamed.

This imparts feelings of negativity and self-loathing. You have zero confidence. Besides, as my friend said, "I don't know why you are always looking at the ground. There's nothing down there but dirt."

He was right. When I began keeping my head up, I was looking at the faces of those passing me by. I found that looking up to the sky was more positive than dragging my gaze along the rocks. Eye contact not only builds confidence, but it makes you feel more honest, outgoing, and connected.

So why are we avoiding eye contact? It creates a feeling of vulnerability. If you have rejection issues, you could be afraid that the other person will not respond to your contact. It puts pressure on you to maintain your eye contact. One reason good eye contact makes a difference is because it builds a sense of trust and companionship. People will respond to you more when you appear honest, open, and appreciative when engaging with them.

Most importantly, you are sending a message: "I am good enough. That is why I can look you in the eye." I avoided eye contact for so long because I didn't believe I was good enough. I didn't want people to see that. But they did see it because I was always looking down or away.

So look up. Look high. Keep your head up and see the people you are engaging with.

Confident eye contact strategy #1 — Look people in the eye with a gentle, approachable expression. Eye contact doesn't have to be a staring contest. This could make people feel uncomfortable, so don't overdo it. Maintain eye contact when you are speaking, gradually looking away when you have to search for a thought, and then make contact again.

Confident eye contact strategy #2 — We are not going for a dominating or overpowering effect here. Think of it as therapy. You want to connect with those you feel uncomfortable around. Your eye contact isn't an intense gaze as if you have something to prove.

You don't want to come across as challenging. Keep it gentle. Add your smile. Be personable. If you want instant likability, these three attitudes combined will attract more opportunity and raise your self-esteem levels considerably.

While it is important to have people react to our confident positivity, what we are really going after is boosting our internal feelings of self-esteem. We want that "feel good" approach that we are good enough. If you do it for others, you will fall into the trap of people-pleasing to be liked, and if you get a negative reaction it will fall back and trigger your negative validation all over again.

You can keep your eye intensity to a minimum. Look confident but interested. Appear relaxed but alert.

Confident eye contact strategy #3 — Our eyes really are the windows to the deeper parts of ourselves. They may be the windows to the soul, but more importantly, they indicate how you feel about yourself. One look into someone's eyes can tell you a lot about a person.

My former mentor, who was a top salesperson in his company, would say, "If you can't look someone in the eye when they are engaged with you, they are not going to buy anything. The first thing we teach people, new recruits, is to look people in the eye if you want a sale. It was shocking how difficult this was for many of our recruits."

Positive Body Movements

Positive body language can be defined as nonverbal movements and gestures that are communicating interest, enthusiasm, and **positive** reactions to what some else is saying.

By now, you may start to recognize some of the negative messages you send out about yourself just by observing your own body language. We know that by controlling the way we move, we can regulate our emotions. Confidence is more than just the way you think; that's only part of it. Confidence is a reaction to how you behave. If you act confidently, you'll feel more vibrant and empowered. It is natural.

People can tell a lot about you and the language you communicate through body movements. Your body language includes hand positioning, stance, and facial expressions. This is non-verbal communication that tells a story about your level of confidence and self-esteem. Those who are highly tuned-in may be able to tell what you are feeling at the moment.

But these are not the reasons why posing as a confident person is important. We are not looking to impress anyone here. Our main purpose with eye contact and body language is not to just appear confident, but to feel confident and in control of our emotions, working toward eliminating fears of social interaction.

You will create a powerful positive mindset when you practice body language focused on positive movements that generates interest, expresses intelligence, and puts you into the right mindset for acting out with enthusiasm.

Why Body Language Matters

The focus of this book is on feeling great about ourselves and reclaiming the personal power that we have lost along the way. For those who've never experienced or developed that personal power to begin with, this is your chance to shine and become someone who attracts instead of repels.

Basically, your internal emotions control to a larger extent how you present yourself on the outside. Your external world will always reflect the inner you. You can try to hide and fake your way through appearing that you have it together, but the game won't last forever. It is also exhausting trying to be something you're not.

First of all, the weak postures that people with low self-esteem and loads of fear portray are:

- Folding your arms (defensive and protective)

- Touching your face/neck (appearing nervous or uncomfortable)

- Hands in pockets

- Keeping your distance

- Eyes downcast or off to the side (lacking confidence and expressing shame)

- Low tone, unclear voice (lacking confidence and expressing fear in saying the wrong thing)

The positive positioning that will boost your overall confidence and make you unstoppable are:

- Smile

- Wide and expressive gestures

- A calm and positive manner

- Inviting people into your personal space

How I Used to Present Myself

Body language was never my strong point, and I never equated it with feeling good about myself. But after picking up on the techniques of presenting myself with greater confidence in front of others, it changed the way I felt inside as well. Your internal and external emotions are connected. You don't have to fake it till you make it. You should act the way you want to feel. It just makes sense.

For years, I walked around with my head down, I didn't smile much, and I was always crossing my arms and keeping people at a distance. This is how I felt on the inside as well—sad, depressed, lacking self-esteem and confidence. As my internal emotions healed, my external appearance showed improvement but I still acted like someone who had a lot of negativity inside. So, I put into practice the tips that follow.

Wear a Smile

We all know smiling is awesome, but people who are trapped in self-defeating behaviors struggle to convey any real happiness. We feel bad about ourselves, and so we act the part. Smiling can change everything for you in an instant. It reduces stress and it's a positive form of communication. People see that and they want to talk to you, be your friend, and open their doors to you. Smiling brings opportunity. It conveys that you're not only happy, but you are a person who feels good about themselves.

You don't have to walk around with a permanent smile on your face, so choose the time and place. You can practice it when you're alone. Smiling stretches your facial muscles and adds depth to your complexion. What's more, it makes others feel good.

My father smiled often. He hated business meetings and had to join them regularly. The atmosphere was always stiff and serious, so he added an element of humor to the meeting. He'd smile, tell a joke, and lighten the mood. It worked because the CEO of the company asked him to join all of the meetings after that because he couldn't stand the atmosphere the other executives were creating with their solemn expressions and angry vocals.

My father, who suffered from his own demons and struggled with self-defeating thoughts and behaviors, had the ability to make others feel welcome and relaxed through smiling and expressing himself in a positive way. He figured out that if you want to change the way you feel, you can work on helping others change the way *they* feel.

Here's what you can do:

1. In the morning, work on smiling for ten minutes. Make it a morning exercise just like any other exercise routine.

2. Smile when you're around your children or other loved ones. Let them know it's important.

Your Hands and Arms

In combination with your confident eye contact and a powerful smile, your hands and arms are the third element to positive and confident body language.

Have you ever watched someone do a Ted Talk or listened to a keynote speaker? Have you ever watched the legendary Steve Jobs deliver a presentation? If so, you know these people don't have their hands in their pockets and they're not folding their arms. I'll be the first to admit these have always been relaxed positions for me, but when it comes to communicating, they appear weak, defensive, and can convey negativity.

This doesn't mean we shouldn't ever do it. Do whatever feels comfortable but do it for yourself first and foremost. When I cross my arms, for example, I feel superior, defensive or self-righteous. I don't like this, so I made myself aware of it.

Instead, I became more expressive with my hands and arms. This makes others feel energized and it also changes how I feel inside. Remember that every action you take, every body movement, and the language you use will either empower or disempower you.

Here is what we can do: Imitate the people who move with confidence, assurance, and positive body language. Watch how they react and express their emotions. Through imitating others, we can attain similar results and eventually find our own style of communicating.

Your Life on Relaunch: Building the Master Vision

"Do not give up your dream because it is apparently not being realized, because you cannot see it coming true. Cling to your vision with all the tenacity you can muster. Keep it bright; do not let the bread-and-butter side of life cloud your ideal or dim it."

— Orison Swett Marden

We are near the end of the book, but before we finish, I've saved this for last: **building a vision for your life**. Now you are going to take massive action and create real opportunity for growth. Through creating a visual concept of the ideal life you want, you can move out of the past and guide your thoughts towards focusing on the positive changes in your life.

Visual Pathways to Success

The only obstacle that's holding you back at this point is yourself. We know the blame game is over. We have looked at the reasons why we're trapped in a life of self-defeat. Now we know how to heal the past and forge a life with a better future in which we can be happy, fulfilled, and loved. We are no longer hung up on our shortcomings or failures, and we are not using these as leverage to gain sympathy.

Building a vision for yourself should be a daily habit. I spend twenty minutes a day working on my life vision. This habit, when practiced, makes you focused. It details the steps needed to take action. Instead of thinking about your hurts and grievances, you are focusing on the dreams you can build.

When focusing on a vision, such as the new you five years from now, it is impossible to stay focused on the past. Your soul wants to explore the unknown potential you have been hiding for so long. It's time to let your imagination go and tap into your creative flow.

The Growing Pains of Desire

As you work toward something you really want, you might experience feelings of shame, regret, or guilt for wanting something. You spent a lot of years wanting the things that would make you happy, but you felt guilty for voicing those needs.

When we feel low about ourselves, it's a heavy challenge to raise ourselves up. But now we know that we can envision, dream, plan, and take massive action toward the life that is to be ours.

Here's what **Michelle** said:

> "I spent years training myself to feel good about who I was. Then, one day, it suddenly hit me. I wasn't living my life, but the life of all the people who had controlled me and kept me from reaching my greatest potential. When I started to recover, I

remember feeling really angry. Like I wanted them to know how much damage had been done. But then someone told me, 'The people you are angry at are still living their lives. They don't care about your feelings. If you don't move on, you'll have wasted everything by hating. Do what you've always wanted to do.' And so I did."

We know life isn't always fair. As we learned in this book, everyone has a past and we are taking the best possible path we know. But the people who end up with heavy regret and remain stuck are those who are trapped in worry, fear, uncertainty, and thoughts about past failures. Those who make it and forge a greater lifestyle cut the cords, take responsibility, and plan out the life they never had.

The choice is yours. You can build the vision you've always wanted or continue to relive the memories that no longer serve you.

That brings us to building the vision for your life.

20 Questions: Mapping Out Your Vision

By mapping out your master vision, you are laying the critical stepping-stones on the path that defines why you are here; it creates the steps for what needs to be done to bring your dream to life. Just as the carpenter builds the framework of a house with the proper tools for the job, this aims to provide you with some useful tools to construct the foundation of your life.

Take some time to ask yourself these questions. Be as detailed as you can. Before you write anything, take some time to consider you answers. Do a mental brainstorm and then commit your answer to paper.

Imagine how you would live each day if you were doing exactly what you wanted. These questions will forge the framework of your life's vision.

1. If you could have anything in this world, what would it be?

2. How would you live each day if you knew it was to be your last?

3. Five years from now, where would you like to be professionally, financially, and spiritually?

4. Make a list of the limiting beliefs that you have been holding on to. What actions can you take today to eliminate these limiting beliefs from your life?

5. What experiences do you visualize yourself having? Is it traveling? Starting your own business?

6. What is your lifelong goal? What kind of person would you have to become to achieve this lifelong goal?

7. What are your greatest values right now? What values would you have to develop in your life to successfully live your dream?

8. What obstacles are you facing and how will you overcome them? Take time now to mind map your solutions.

9. What resources are available to you to help you succeed? How often do you tap into these resources?

10. What kind of people would have to connect with you in order to make your dreams a reality?

11. Imagine yourself at the end of your life. What stage of progress have you reached with your goals? What steps do you have to take to reach your objective?

12. What would you have done differently in your life if you had the opportunity? What will you do differently from this day forward?

13. What do you think is the specific character defect holding you back from pursuing your life's work? What methods could you adopt to overcome this character defect? If you were to overcome this, how would your life be different?

14. What character trait would you need to adopt so that you could achieve your master vision?

15. Write down the names of three people who influence you the most. What is it about these people you admire?

16. Where would you like to spend the rest of your life?

17. Who would you like to spend the rest of your life with?

18. What are the interests and passions that you feel completely bound to? What do you feel compelled to do?

19. If you knew that you could not fail, what would you do right now? If you had no limiting thoughts and all negative concepts were suddenly washed away, what would you do now? Would it be the one thing you have always been afraid to try?

20. Looking back at who you were five, 10, or 20 years ago, how has your life progressed? Are you a different person today? If so, how have you changed? If not, what changes could you now implement?

If you have taken the time to answer these questions, you have just set in motion a powerful stream of visual consciousness. You can focus on what matters the most by knowing yourself on a deeper level from the inside. By knowing what you really want in life, you will place yourself in the top percentage of successful achievers.

Now, consider this: how would you feel physically, mentally, and emotionally if you were to succeed at achieving this one goal, your **Master Goal**, in your life? Would you have more money, more freedom, or the capacity to create a global network of connections and friendships? Whatever it may be, however crazy or impossible it may sound, write down your goal. Define it in writing and make it real.

When you seek to build your dreams, you can take comfort in knowing everything you have ever wanted is being created in the here and now. All the opportunities you have ever needed are available today. How you live all your days from this one to the last has unlimited potential and plays a significant role in the larger picture of your life.

Continue to think deeply, clearly, and creatively about the life you are going to live. Let nothing deter you or break your level of concentration. Know precisely what it is you want and make a plan for achieving it. See your life as a blueprint for success.

Repeatedly envision that you have already succeeded and it will become a reality. Imagine the positive outcomes that your daily progressive thoughts and actions have created. See yourself as the great person you desire to become and then be that person from today onward. Invest all your actions, visions, and thoughts toward achieving your master vision.

Conclusion: The Joy of Freedom

"In order to carry a positive action, we must develop here a positive vision."

— Dalai Lama

There is nothing more rewarding than a life well-lived. This book is a stepping-stone to a new level of freedom. Enough with the life half-lived in which we let others determine how good we are. From now on, it is up to each of us to decide how much we are worth, and to recognize that nobody else is qualified to make that decision.

Brene Brown, the New York Times bestselling author of *Rising Strong*, said: *"Because true belonging only happens when we present our authentic, imperfect selves to the world, our sense of belonging can never be greater than our level of self-acceptance."*

I'll leave you with these seven tips on recovery and how you can continue working on yourself. The journey doesn't end when we start to feel a little better. There is always another peak to aim for. I want you to keep pushing for that place you're afraid to go.

1. Don't go it alone.

I can't stress this enough: Make good friends along the way and connect with people who love, support, and encourage you. It goes both ways. When it comes to the people who are holding you back or demeaning you, the time has come to make some tough choices. If they're close family, you may have to have some form of relationship with them. But you don't have to let them decide what that is.

You draw the boundary and let them know what the rules are. When we act with passive uncertainty, it gives them the chance to control our emotional state. We can control that and we are in charge of our own affairs. So, stay close to the people you need, and who need you.

2. Make change a lifelong habit.

Relaunching your lifestyle isn't a default experience. To make real changes that stick, we have to be intentional with our habits. This means choosing the habits that drive the actions to get the results we want.

Persevere and continue to stay focused on the patterns you want to change. It won't happen overnight but the changes you seek will develop over time.

Set out each week to tackle one specific area. If you are struggling with rejection issues and this is your core area of self-defeat, then do something to break the cycle. Get into the habit of asking for one thing a day.

Create a task list that gets you to take action. This doesn't have to be a massive project. Drive yourself to improve in the area of your life that is causing you the most grief. Focus on accomplishing a small task. This can be a small goal until you feel comfortable tackling larger challenges.

3. Be Relentless in Your Pursuit of Happiness.

Happiness comes and goes. It is like any relationship: you have to continuously work at it to keep it thriving. Focus on long-term assets that build a happy life through relationships, work, and of course, the quality of your mental health. By sticking to a plan that brings us new pockets of joy, our future will be a positive one to look forward to.

We have to continuously work at bringing happiness into our lives. On those days when we struggle with life's complexities, we can choose to fall under the burden, or rise above it. Be relentless in going after what draws unlimited positivity towards you. In doing so, we will leave our old, worn-out habits behind and foster better habits that drive us towards success.

4. Look at the reality of your situation.

James Stockdale was a United States Vice Admiral who was shot down in 1965 and held as a prisoner of war in Vietnam for over seven years. While captive he was routinely tortured and made to undergo some of the harshest treatments any person could endure.

When asked how he made it through alive, while other prisoners around him died, Stockdale said: "Oh, that's easy, the optimists. Oh, they were the ones who said, 'We're going to be out by Christmas.' And Christmas would come, and Christmas would go. Then they'd say, 'We're going to be out by Easter.' And Easter would come, and Easter would go. And then Thanksgiving, and then it would be Christmas again. And they died of a broken heart."

It goes without saying that confronting the brutal facts of your reality, no matter how terrifying, is smarter that convincing yourself it's okay when in your heart you know it really isn't.

By sticking with the reality of your situation, you can figure out the best way to handle it. As we learned in Chapter 4, avoidance of our situation is what makes it fester and grow worse. The situation that has power over you is the situation that control or kills you. As James Stockdale observed, the men who couldn't accept their situation as it was, died from despair.

While you may not be in such a dire situation, when you face a difficulty you might be anxious, scared and tempted to avoid it. That is when you can decide to do things differently. Transcend your fear by taking forward action. Any small step will be much better than nothing.

Ask yourself what you are losing by avoiding this critical step. Stay grounded in reality and you will have cured anxiety and fear for the most part. Both of these are grounded in keeping us scared.

5. Continue to develop your vision.

As Helen Keller once said: "The only thing worse than being blind is having sight but no vision."

You can forge the life you want and launch your life again and again by continuously updating the vision for your life. When we stop visualizing the life we want for ourselves, we end up living someone else's dream.

In Chapter 12, we covered vision building and how to define what you really want for your life. When we set ourselves on the course of healing, something transformative takes over and we start to become different people.

Your vision is the master blueprint for your life. Spend ten minutes a day cultivating this vision. Add to it. Have fun with it. Visualize the life you always wanted and create only the best thoughts so you can get it.

6. Express your needs with aggressive intention.

When you express what you want with intentional confidence, people listen. You don't have to confuse this with a demanding child who cries for what they want, but as an adult who is finally carving out his or her place and needs to be heard.

As we learned in an earlier chapter on rejection, asking for what we want is a big obstacle to get over. But now that we know it works, we can ask for anything we desire—more love, money, or we can ask someone to stop treating us in a way that's detrimental to us.

7. Reconnect with the inner child.

As we know, many of the fears, insecurities, and feelings of vulnerability we experience can be traced back to our lives as children. That inner child still wants to communicate, even if we may have pushed him or her away in our attempt to live a normal life.

Several years ago, I started to reconnect with the memories of my childhood. I would visualize walking into a room with my younger self and having a conversation with this person. It is a very empowering activity. When he was frightened or feeling vulnerable, I would visit and console this person. This is one of the best cognitive activities for connecting with your inner child who went through so much.

In connecting, we can heal the past that has been closed and instead of avoiding all the stuff that was forgotten, we can bring it out into the open. It is amazing what you will discover about yourself and the truth.

As someone said to me, "Once I realized that I was no longer a victim, and that I could talk back to the voices and say no to the abusive words or behavior, it changed the perspective completely. I could reinvent the memory and turn it into a point of power instead of feeling sorry for myself."

By reading this book, I hope you gained some knowledge and wisdom—enough to go out there and make a difference, not in just your own life, but in the lives of many others.

Don't put off living for one more day.

And always...

Pass on what you have learned so you can help others.

Stay focused on a path of consistent and never-ending self-improvement.

All the best on your journey,

Scott Allan

"Mastery, I learned, was not something genetic, or for a lucky few. It is something we can all attain if get rid of some misconceptions and gain clarity as to the required path."

— **Robert Greene**

Books Change Lives.
Let's Change Yours Today.

Check out the complete
<u>Bulletproof Mindset Mastery series</u> here by Scott Allan.

The **Rejection Free for Life**
Series Books

Begin Your Rejection Free Journey Today!
RejectionFreeBooks.com

Pathways to Mastery Series

Master Your Life One Book at a Time

Available where eBooks, books and audiobooks are sold.

About Scott Allan

Scott Allan is an international bestselling author of 25+ books published in 9 languages in the area of personal growth and self-development. He is the author of **Fail Big, Undefeated,** and **Do the Hard Things First**.

As a former corporate business trainer in Japan, and **Transformational Mindset Strategist**, Scott has invested over 10,000 hours of research and instructional coaching into the areas of self-mastery and leadership training.

With an unrelenting passion for teaching, building critical life skills, and inspiring people around the world to take charge of their lives, Scott Allan is committed to a path of **constant and never-ending self-improvement**.

Many of the success strategies and self-empowerment material that is reinventing lives around the world evolves from Scott Allan's 20 years of practice and teaching critical skills to corporate executives, individuals, and business owners.

You can connect with Scott at:

scottallan@scottallanpublishing.com

Visit author.to/ScottAllanBooks to stay up to date on future book releases.

Scott Allan

Master Your Life One Book at a Time.

<u>Subscribe</u> to the weekly newsletter for actionable content and updates on future book releases from Scott Allan.